10 Women Who Changed the World

Inspiring Female
Missionaries
Who Fulfilled
the Great Commission

10 Women Who Changed the World

DANIEL L. AKIN

Printed in the United States of America

978-1-0877-8743-5

Published by B&H Publishing Group
Brentwood, Tennessee

Dewey Decimal Classification: 266.092
Subject Heading: MISSIONARIES / MISSIONS / WOMEN MISSIONARIES

Cover design by Darren Welch.
Cover image by Andrea Mazzocchetti / Alamy Stock Photo.
Additional images arigato/Shutterstock and faestock/Shuttrestock.

1 2 3 4 5 • 27 26 25 24

This book is dedicated to all of the wonderful women whose love for Christ and the nations compelled them to go, often at great cost and sacrifice, wherever He led. They are heroes to me and their lives are worthy of honor and imitation. May more go because of the inspiration found from their lives.

Acknowledgments

This book would not have been written without the incredible support and encouragement of Ashley Gorman and Devin Maddox (B&H), Kim Humphrey, Devin Moncada, and Kimberly Rochelle (SEBTS). You guys are simply the best and I thank you all for walking with me in this project.

Contents

Introduction

Jim Elliot wrote in a letter to his parents, "Missionaries are very human folks, just doing what they are asked. Simply a bunch of nobodies trying to exalt Somebody."[1]

I have no doubt the ten women whose stories are recounted in this book would agree with Jim Elliot's assessment. In comparison to the glorious Savior we serve, we are all a bunch of nobodies. And yet, in Christ, our identity is radically changed, and our worth to the heavenly Father is beautifully brought to light. Nobodies become sons and daughters of the King of heaven, and our lives take on a new significance of eternal value and worth. What God does in us and through us is nothing less than supernatural.

As I have studied missions and read missionary biographies over my lifetime, I have been amazed and inspired by the large number of women who left home, families, comfort, and safety in obedience to Jesus and his command to go to the nations with his gospel. Their number is far greater than most realize, and often their names disappeared in the mist of history. That reality is a great loss to the church of King Jesus. In this book, I attempt to recover at least ten of their stories.

In terms of how I approach each woman's story, I follow the pattern of my previous missionary book *Ten Who Changed the World*. I wed the lives and writings of these servants of Christ to a biblical text they exemplify. This approach allows us to both study the biblical text and see the story of ten women whose lives made a difference for the advance of the gospel among the nations.

Words are inadequate to express how my own life has been impacted by these ten women. My prayer is our Lord will use my meager effort in telling their stories to inspire many more of his servants to help the unreached and unengaged hear the good news of the Lamb who was slain and raised from the dead for them.

May Carl F. H. Henry's words continually ring in our ears: "The gospel is only good news if it gets there in time."[2] These ladies gave their lives to see it get there in time. May we all follow their example.

God Knows What He Is Doing–
Beautifully Exemplified in the Life of

Sarah Hall Boardman Judson[1]

PSALM 138

Sarah Hall Boardman Judson (1803–1845) was a remarkable Christian missionary who faithfully served King Jesus in Burma (modern Myanmar) for over twenty years. She married and buried one missionary husband (George Boardman) and then remarried and was buried by another (Adoniram Judson). Her life was a marvelous witness both to the grace of God and to the wisdom of God. Her life testifies that our God knows what he is doing even during the greatest difficulties and trials. Her life is also a beautiful commentary on a thanksgiving psalm of King David, Psalm 138, a psalm with Messianic overtones.[2]

This psalm has four movements (vv. 1–2, 3, 4–6, 7–8). It will be a journey of joy and sorrow to see the life of Sarah B. Judson reflected in its truth. Sarah's life was one of absolute confidence in a sovereign Savior, a confidence that enabled her to pen this hymn:

Proclaim the lofty praise
Of Him who once was slain,
But now is risen, through endless days,
To live and reign.
He lives and reigns on high,
Who bought us with His blood,
Enthroned above the farthest sky,
Our Savior, God.[3]

Thank God for Who He Is before the Nations

(PSALM 138:1–2)

David sounds the praise of thanksgiving from the beginning of this psalm, "I will give you thanks with all my heart." And where will David herald his thanksgiving? He says, "I will sing your praise before the heavenly beings" (v. 1). The meaning of this last phrase is not clear and is also translated as "before the gods" (so ESV) or "before judges" or "before kings" (see the translation note in the CSB). Allen Ross favors the translation "before the gods" and writes, "Other passages in this part of the Psalter refer to pagan gods as well (Pss. 95:3; 96:4–5; and 115:3–8). The psalmist praises the greatness and glory of Yahweh 'in the face'—so to speak, of false gods."[4] We prefer this understanding. Verse 2 expands the thought of verse 1, explaining just how David will testify and sing his thanksgiving of the Lord before these false gods. He will "bow down toward [God's] holy temple [or tabernacle]" in Jerusalem. There he will "give thanks to [the Lord's] name for your constant love [Heb. *hesed*] and truth [Heb. *emeth*, ESV "faithfulness"]." And why will he bow down and sing of the Lord's love and truth, his "steadfast love and faithfulness"

(ESV)? Because "you [the LORD] have exalted your name and your promise (ESV, "your word") above everything else." Commenting on this verse, Charles Spurgeon writes,

> The name of the Lord in nature is not so easily read as in the Scriptures, which are a revelation in human language, specifically adapted to the human mind, treating of human need, and of a Saviour who appeared in human nature to redeem humanity. Heaven and earth shall pass away, but the divine word will not pass away, and in this respect especially it has a pre-eminence over every other form of manifestation. Moreover, the Lord lays all the rest of his name under tribute to his word: his wisdom, power, love, and all his other attributes combine to carry out his word. It is his word which creates, sustains, quickens, enlightens, and comforts. As a word of command it is supreme; and in the person of the incarnate Word it is set above all the works of God's hand. . . . Let us adore the Lord who has spoken to us by his word, and by his Son; and in the presence of unbelievers let us both praise his holy name and extol his holy word.[5]

If ever there was a follower of the Lord Jesus who praised the name of the Savior and extolled his gospel before the lost and their false gods, it was Sarah B. Judson. Sarah was born on November 4, 1803, in Alstead, New Hampshire. She was the oldest of thirteen children in a family that was extremely poor. At the age of seventeen, she was converted, professed Christ, and was baptized. She felt the call to missions immediately and wished "to follow in the footsteps of her heroine Ann Judson, who visited America in 1823."[6] In the book *Missionary Biography. The Memoir of Sarah B. Judson, Member of the American Mission to Burmah*, Emily Judson (pen name Fanny Forester), the third and last wife of Adoniram Judson, includes an entry from Sarah's journal written less than a month after her baptism. There Sarah writes, "While I have this day had the privilege of worshipping the true God in solemnity, I have been pained by the thoughts of those who have never heard the sound of the gospel. When will the time come that the poor heathen, now bowing to idols, shall own the living and true God? Dear Saviour, haste to spread the knowledge of thy dying love to earth's remotest bounds!"[7]

Her passion for the lost would continue to grow. She became involved in tract distribution and established a prayer meeting. All but one who attended became Christians. However, her heart for the nations would not wane. In a letter to a dear friend she would write,

> It is my ardent desire . . . that the glorious work of reformation may extend till *every knee* shall bow to the living God. For this expected, this promised era, let us pray earnestly, unceasingly, and with faith. How can I be so inactive, when I know that thousands are perishing in this land of grace; and millions in other lands are at this very moment kneeling before senseless idols!

And in her journal—

> Sinners perishing all round me, and I almost panting to tell the far *heathen* of Christ! Surely this is wrong. I will no longer indulge the vain foolish wish, but endeavor to be useful in the position where Providence has placed me. I can *pray* for deluded idolaters, and for those who labor among them, and this is a privilege indeed.[8]

Sarah, however, could not shake loose her concern for the lost who were far away. Her heart for international missions would find a companion in a man named George Boardman. Moved by a poem he read on the death of a missionary named Colman, who died in Chittagong after only two years on the field, Boardman tracked down its author, who happened to be Sarah Hall. He proposed to her almost immediately, and she accepted. Initially, her friends and family discouraged her in this action, with her parents withholding their consent. Eventually, however, they gave their permission. George and Sarah wed on July 4, 1825. They would leave for Burma the same month, and the voyage would take 127 days. The moving scene of their departure, never to return, is one of the most heart-wrenching in all missionary lore. Sarah's departure is recorded in this way:

> We recollect that when she left her paternal home, to reach the ship which was to convey her "over the dark and distant sea," after she had taken her seat in the stage coach with her chosen companion . . . and had bestowed her last farewell upon the family group—as though she felt that she had not obtained that free and full consent to her abandonment of home and country which her filial heart craved, she looked out at the coach window and said, "Father, are you willing? Say, father, that you are willing I should go." "Yes, my child, I am willing." "Now I can go joyfully!" was the emphatic response; and the noble wanderer went on her way with cheerful composure.
>
> Of this scene [Sarah] writes to her husband's parents, "My mother embraced me as tenderly, when she whispered, 'Sarah, I hope I am willing,' as she

did one month before, when she wildly said, 'Oh! I cannot part with you!'"[9]

Fanny then adds to this sorrowful scene:

And so the fond child's heart was made glad even in the moment of its agony; for something of the previous reluctance of the sorrow-stricken parents to resign their treasure may be gathered from such pleadings as these [from Sarah].

"Let us, my dear parents, go to Calvary; let us behold for a few moments, the meek, the holy Lamb of God, bleeding for our transgressions. Then let us inquire, 'Shall I withhold from this Saviour any object, however dear to my heart? Shall I be unwilling to suffer a few short years of toil and privation for his sake?' Let us call to remembrance those days of darkness through which we passed before Jesus lifted upon us the light of his countenance. We have, I trust, each of us, seen our lost and ruined condition by nature, have seen ourselves exposed to the righteous indignation of our Creator, have felt ourselves sinking into endless despair and ruin, and all this is merited. But oh, amazing love! at that desperate moment the Saviour smiled upon us. He opened his arms of compassion, all polluted as we were with iniquity, he received us, forgave our sins, and bade us hope for joy unutterable beyond the grave. Did we not, then, surrender *all* into his hand? Was not this the language of our hearts,

'Had I a thousand lives to give,
A thousand lives should all be thine!'

> And has not the precious Redeemer as strong claims upon us now as he had then?"[10]

May we, like David and like Sarah, thank God and proclaim his love and faithfulness before the nations and their false gods so that they too may worship and sing praises to our Lord!

Thank God That He Answers Prayers as We Witness

(PSALM 138:3)

Verse 3 naturally flows out of verses 1–2. David praised and thanked God for his constant love and faithfulness because, at an unspecified time when David sought the Lord ("On the day I called"), "you answered me." Furthermore, the answer included "increased strength within me." Alec Motyer words this verse as, "You invigorate me with strength in my soul."[11] Within his inner being, the Lord gave David strength, courage, and boldness as he rejoiced in the Lord before pagan gods and their idolatrous followers. This work is certainly something God did for Sarah Boardman Judson.

Unsurprisingly, Sarah would experience many hardships on the mission field. More than once she nearly died from severe sickness. Giving birth to three children with George, only one (George Jr.) would survive infancy. On more than one occasion, her life was put in danger by robbery of her home, riots, and rebellions. Indeed, she was warned by an English general of "lawless men and the wild beasts of the jungle" in Burma.[12] Yet in her journal, Sarah would write,

> We trembled when we thought of the disturbances in Burmah, and there was only one spot where we could

> find peace and serenity of mind. That sweet spot was the throne of grace. [There] we would often [go] and lose all anxiety and fear respecting our dear friends, our own future prospects, and the Missionary cause in Burmah. It was sweet to commit all into the hands of God. . . . We considered it our duty to supplicate for grace to support us in the hour of trial, and for direction in time of perplexity.[13]

And, after the robbery in their home while they lay in bed at night, Sarah would recount the kind provision and protection of God in their lives. She writes,

> I saw the assassins with their horrid weapons standing by our bedside, ready to do their worst had we been permitted to wake. Oh how merciful was that watchful Providence which prolonged those powerful slumbers of that night, not allowing even the infant at my bosom to open its eyes at so critical a moment. If ever gratitude glowed in my bosom, if ever the world appeared to me worthless as vanity, and if ever I wished to dedicate myself, my husband, my babe, my *all*, to our great Redeemer, it was at that time. . . .
>
> Yes, my beloved friend, I think I can say, that notwithstanding our alarms, never did five months of my life pass as pleasantly as the last five have done. The thought of being among this people whom we have so long desired to see, and the hope that God would enable me to do some little good to the poor heathen, has rejoiced and encouraged my heart. I confess that once or twice my natural timidity has *for a moment* gained ascendancy over my better

> feelings. . . . But these fears have been transitory, and we have generally been enabled to place our confidence in the Great Shepherd of Israel who never slumbers or sleeps, assured that he would protect us. . . . And we have also felt a sweet composure in the reflection that God has marked out our way; and if it best accord with his designs that we fall prey to these blood-thirsty monsters, *all will be right.*[14]

Thank God That He Blesses the Humble but Rejects the Proud

(PSALM 138:4–6)

Verses 4–6 contain what Allen Ross calls "a prophecy concerning the nations."[15] I call it a "missionary promise!" All the nations, represented by their kings, "will give you thanks, LORD, when they hear what you promised" (v. 4; see also Ps. 68:29–32; 72:10–11; 102:15–16). This language anticipates and echoes Isaiah 52:15 and the great Suffering Servant song (Isa. 52:13–53:12). When the kings of the earth hear of the great salvation of God on their behalf through his Servant, "they will sing of the LORD's ways," joyfully acknowledging that "the LORD's glory is great" (v. 5). Here salvation (v. 4) and adoration (v. 5) are beautifully woven together.

The glory of the Lord is further made known when you consider that "though [he] is exalted, he takes note of the humble" (v. 6; cf. Phil. 2:9–11). The Lord sees the down and out, the nobodies of this world, and they become the objects of his saving goodness and grace. In contrast, "He knows the haughty from a distance." God *is* great, and the arrogant only *think* they are great. The humble he knows lovingly and intimately. The arrogant, the prideful, and the self-righteous, he keeps at arm's length. "A glance from afar," says Spurgeon, "reveals to him their emptiness and offensiveness . . . he has no respect unto them, but utterly abhors them."[16]

The Burmese, awash in pagan religions, were proud and self-righteous. It would take a patient, steady stream of gospel truth to break through this barrier. God sent the Judsons and Boardmans to do just that. God brought a notorious Karen criminal and murderer—it is reported he was involved in more than thirty murders—Ko Thah-Byoo, to faith in Jesus. George Boardman would baptize him, and Ko Thah-Byoo would become a famous and successful evangelist among the Karen people. The gospel began to go forth in great power. It appears God had prepared the Karen for the day of their salvation. In their tradition, "they believe in a God who is denominated Yu-wah."[17] Though they recognized that their wickedness had separated them from this God, they believed "God will again have mercy upon us, God will save us again."[18] When will that day come? In one of their traditional songs, we read this verse, "When the Karen King arrives, / Everything will be happy; / When Karens have a king, / Wild beast will lose their savageness."[19] Reflecting upon the grace of God among the Karen, but recognizing there was still much work to be done, Sarah would write to a beloved sister in 1828, "We have to suffer many little inconveniences in this country; but have no disposition to complain. We rejoice in the kind providence that has directed our steps, and would not exchange our condition. Our desire is to labor among the poor heathen until called to our eternal home."[20]

God would indeed answer this desire of Sarah's heart. Both George and she would die on the mission field never having returned to America. Thank God He blesses humble servants.

Thank God That He Will Fulfill His Purpose in Your Life

(PSALM 138:7–8)

This psalm concludes with a powerful confession of confidence in the providence, protection, and grace of a sovereign God. Five affirmations are made concerning the God who is with us. "If I walk into the thick of danger, [God] will . . . not abandon the work of [his] hands" (vv. 7–8). What does David declare in terms of his confidence in the Lord?

> You will preserve my life from the anger of my
> enemies.
> You will extend your hand [i.e., your power and
> strength];
> your right hand will save me.
> The LORD will fulfill his purpose for me.
> LORD, your faithful love endures forever. (vv. 7–8)

These faithful promises apply so appropriately and beautifully in the life of Sarah Boardman Judson. God would spare her life on more than one occasion from serious illness. He would sustain her heart upon the death of her little daughter Sarah on July 8, 1829—she was two years and eight months. And he would preserve her as she watched her husband slowly descend into death from tuberculosis. Of this time, she would write to her mother, "Oh, my dear mother, it would distress you to see how emaciated he is!—and so weak, that he is scare able to move. God is calling to me in a most impressive manner to set my heart on heavenly things. Two lovely infants already in the world of bliss—my beloved husband suffering under a disease which will most assuredly take him from me—my own health poor, and little Georgie [their son] often ill."[21]

George Boardman would die on February 11, 1831, at the age of thirty. Of her first husband Sarah said, "He exhibited a tenderness of spirit, a holy sensibility, such as I never witnessed before. He seemed to see the goodness of God in everything. He would weep while conversing on the love of Jesus; and words cannot describe to you the depth of feeling with which he spoke of his own unworthiness."[22]

As he neared death, Sarah reports him saying, "You know, Sarah, that coming on a foreign mission involves the probability of a shorter life than staying in one's native country. And yet obedience to our Lord, and compassion for the perishing heathen, induced us to make this sacrifice. And have we ever repented that we came? No; I trust we can both say that we bless God for bringing us to Burmah, for directing our footsteps to Tavoy, and even for leading us hither."[23]

After George's death, Sarah at first considered returning to America with her young son, but her love for the Burmese compelled her to stay.

She wrote,

> When I first stood by the grave of my husband, I thought I must go home with George. But these poor, inquiring, and Christian Karens, and the school-boys, and the Burmese Christians, would then be left without any one to instruct them; and the poor, [ignorant] Tavoyans would go on in the road to death, with no one to warn them of their danger. How then, oh, how can I go? We shall not be separated long. A few more years, and we shall all meet in yonder blissful world, whither those we

> love have gone before us. I feel thankful that I was allowed to come to this heathen land. Oh, it is a precious privilege to tell idolaters of the Gospel; and when we see them disposed to love the Saviour, we forget all our privations and dangers. My beloved husband wore out his life in this glorious cause; and that remembrance makes me more than ever attached to the work, and the people for whose salvation he laboured till death.[24]

Three years after her husband's death, Sarah Boardman would marry Adoniram Judson. She had not returned home to America as many friends counseled her to do. However, she would, with a broken heart, eventually send her young son George back to America because of health concerns. He would become the much-respected pastor of FBC Philadelphia (1864–1894) and a well-known opponent of slavery. Sarah would remain in Burma, continuing the work, making evangelistic tours, preaching the gospel to men and women when no qualified man was available, and supervising the numerous schools she helped establish. She would translate *The Pilgrim's Progress* into Burmese. She would translate tracts, including the tract "Life of Christ" that her husband Adoniram wrote, and the New Testament into Peguan. Concerning her preaching to both men and women, a point of controversy in her day and ours, her biographer Fanny Forester puts things in their proper perspective:

> But now she sat in the zayat, which had been erected for her husband, at the foot of the mountain, and in others, wherever a little company of worshippers could be collected, and performed even weightier offices than those of Miriam and Anna . . . but meek, and sometimes tearful, speaking in low, gentle

> ascents, and with a manner sweetly persuasive. In several instances she thus conducted the worship of two or three hundred Karens, through the medium of her Burmese interpreter; and such was her modest manner of accomplishing the unusual task, that even the most fastidious were pleased; and a high officer of the English Church, which is well-known to take strict cognizance of irregularities, saw fit to bestow upon her unqualified praise. These acts, however, were not in accordance with her feminine taste or her sense of propriety. The duty, which called her to them, was fashioned by peculiar circumstance; and, as soon as opportunity offered, she gladly relinquished the task in favour of a person better suited to its performance.[25]

Conclusion

Sarah Boardman Judson would be married to missionary Adoniram Judson for eleven years. She would love him and labor alongside him faithfully as she had her first husband George. She would have eight children with him. Five would survive into adulthood.[26] Her obituary faithfully captures Judson's loving opinion of his second wife:

> The Memoir of his first beloved wife [Ann] has been long before the public. It is, therefore, most gratifying to his feelings to be able to say in truth, that the subject of this notice was, in every point of natural and moral excellence, the worthy successor of Ann H. Judson. He constantly thanks God that he has

> been blest with two of the best of wives; he deeply feels that he has not improved those rich blessings as he ought; and it is most painful to reflect, that from the peculiar pressure of the missionary life, he has sometimes failed to treat those dear beings with that consideration, attention, and kindness, which their situation in a foreign heathen land ever demanded.[27]

Sarah became deathly ill, and her plan was to go home to America with the hope she might recover. It was not to be. Adoniram, Sarah, and three of their small children set sail. Although she briefly rebounded, she lapsed in health once again, and it was obvious she would soon die. Sarah went to be with the Savior she so dearly adored and loved at St. Helena in the South Atlantic on September 1, 1845. She was not quite forty-two years old. Biographer Fanny Forester records the final words shared between Adoniram and Sarah:

> A few days before her death, [Adoniram], called her children to her bedside, and said, in their hearing, "I wish, my love, to ask pardon for every unkind word or deed of which I have ever been guilty. I feel that I have, in many instances, failed of treating you with that kindness and affection which you have ever deserved." "Oh!" said she, "you will kill me if you talk so. It is I that should ask pardon of you; and I only want to get well, that I may have an opportunity of making some return for all your kindness, and of showing you how much I love you."
>
> This recollection of her dying bed leads me to say a few words relative to the closing scenes of her life. . . . Her hope had long been fixed on the Rock of Ages, and she had been in the habit of contemplating

> death as neither distant nor undesirable. As it drew near, she remained perfectly tranquil. No shade of doubt, or fear, or anxiety, ever passed over her mind. She had a prevailing preference to depart, and be with Christ. "I am longing to depart," and "what can I want besides?"[28]

A few days later, the time of her departure to go be with Jesus arrived. Her husband provides the details of their joyful and sorrowful separation:

> At two o'clock in the morning, wishing to obtain one more token of recognition, I roused her attention, and said, "Do you still love the Saviour?" "Oh, yes," she replied, "I ever love the Lord Jesus Christ." I said again, "Do you still love me?" She replied in the affirmative, by a peculiar expression of her own. "Then give me one more kiss," and we exchanged that token of love for the last time. Another hour passed,—life continued to recede,—and she ceased to breathe. For a moment I traced her upward flight, and thought of the wonders which were opening to her view. I then closed her sightless eyes, dressed her, for the last time, in the drapery of death, and being quite exhausted with many sleepless nights, I threw myself down and slept. On awaking in the morning, I saw the children standing and weeping around the body of their dear mother.[29]

Sarah would be buried in St. Helena next to another missionary from Ceylon, a Mrs. Chater.

We would be remiss if we did not note that Sarah was an accomplished poet. Thinking in her last days that she might yet cheat death again, it was determined that she would proceed to America with the children and her husband would return to the work in Burma. Contemplating their forthcoming years of separation, perhaps their permanent separation in this life, she wrote the last words she would ever pen to her husband on a scrap of broken paper. Thankfully, they survived and have become famous in the history of missions.

The Parting

We part on this green islet, Love,
Thou for the Eastern main,
I, for the setting sun, Love—
Oh, when to meet again?

My heart is sad for thee, Love,
For lone thy way will be;
And oft thy tears will fall, Love,
For thy children and for me.

The music of thy daughter's voice
Thou'lt miss for many a year,
And the merry shout of thine elder boys,
Thou'lt list in vain to hear.

When we knelt to see our Henry die,
And heard his last faint moan,
Each wiped the tear from the other's eye—
Now, each must weep alone.

My tears fall fast for thee, Love,—
How can I say farewell?

But go;—thy God be with thee, Love,
Thy heart's deep grief to quell!

Yet my spirit clings to thine, Love,
Thy soul remains with me,
And oft we'll hold communion sweet,
O'er the dark and distant sea.

And who can paint our mutual joy,
When, all our wanderings o'er,
We both shall clasp our infants three,
At home, on Burmah's shore.

But higher shall our raptures glow,
On yon celestial plain,
When the loved and parted here below
Meet, ne'er to part again.

Then gird thine armour on, Love,
Nor faint thou by the way,
Till the Boodh shall fall, and Burman's sons
Shall own Messiah's sway.

Forester records this word about Sarah's poem: "'In all the missionary annals,' says the editor of the 'New York Evangelist,' 'there are few things more affecting than this.'"[30]

Success in missions is defined by faithfulness, not numbers. But the faithfulness of Sarah Boardman Judson did result in much fruit. Today there are more than two and a half million Protestant Christians in Myanmar (Burma); there are almost five thousand churches in Myanmar; and Myanmar holds one of the world's largest Baptist communities in the world.[31] Yes, our God knows what He is doing!

Love that Proves We Belong to Jesus—Beautifully Exemplified in the Life and Martyrdom of

Eleanor Chesnut

JOHN 13:34–35

Jesus gave us the Great Commission in Matthew 28:18–20. He also gave us the Great Commandment in Matthew 22:37–40. Both are captured in John 13:34–35 in words our Lord spoke at the Last Supper on the night he was betrayed. Both are also captured in the life of his superlative servant, a medical missionary named Eleanor Chesnut (1868–1905), a woman whose love for Christ and others would be witnessed and sealed by her blood in martyrdom.

We Must Love Others like Jesus Has Loved Us

(JOHN 13:34)

The word *love* appears only twelve times in John 1–12. It appears forty-four times in John 13–21. "I give you a new command," he says in John 13:34, "Love one another. Just as I have loved you, you are also to love one another." Jesus calls this call to love a "new command" because now he calls us to love as *Jesus* has loved us and because of the new messianic community he is forming around God's redemptive love.[1] Jesus's self-sacrificing love radically reshapes how we love one another. Concerning this new command, Don Carson says, "The new commandment is simple enough for a toddler to memorize and appreciate, profound enough that the most mature believers are repeatedly embarrassed at how poorly they comprehend it and put it into practice."[2]

Finding our way to loving others like Jesus loves us is a difficult path, especially for those God has called to travel a difficult and painful road. This was true of missionary Eleanor Chesnut. She was born in Waterloo, Iowa, in 1868. Her father left the family about the time Eleanor was born. When she was three, her mother also died, leaving her in the care of neighbors. Eleanor grew up believing she was a charity case. And as she grew, so did the gnawing resentment she felt over her unfortunate and unfair situation.

Eleanor would later learn about Park College and Academy, a school with a work-study program that would allow her to earn her way through both high school and college.[3] "Friends later described Eleanor as odd, forlorn, unapproachable, proud, and eccentric when she arrived at Park. She was 15 years old, had very little money, and was forced by necessity to wear clothing donated for poor students. She accepted these with much resentment. Because of her pride, she could not feel any gratitude. She was a 'problem student'–outwardly brave and quiet, but inwardly troubled and unhappy. 'Nobody cares where I go or what I do,' she said. 'It makes no difference about me.'"[4]

Park College was a solid Christian institution in the nineteenth century. Students attended chapel three times a day and were expected to be regular in church attendance. As for her experience in becoming a Christian, "though there are no records of the details of her conversion experience . . . Eleanor joined the church during her eight years at Park, and, more importantly, we have a record of the gradual change in her character that is a sign of true faith. The painful experiences of her childhood, instead of causing bitterness, now caused her to have great love and sympathy for others who were suffering."[5]

Eleanor graduated from Park in 1888 at the age of twenty and immediately enrolled in the Women's Medical College in Chicago. She dreamed of becoming a medical missionary, but she often questioned whether she was qualified. Even after serving for nearly ten years in China, she would confide to a friend, "I do not feel that I am spiritual enough to be a missionary."[6]

Eleanor was extremely poor as she began her training; "she lived in an unheated attic and cooked her own meals—mostly oatmeal—and nearly starved the first year. She worked as a nurse during the summers to pay her expenses."[7] Interesting fact of history: "She cared for Oliver Wendell Holmes Sr. in his last illness."[8]

After completing medical school and becoming a doctor, Eleanor attended Moody Bible Institute to prepare for life as a missionary. Her time at Moody was short. In 1894, at the age of 26, she sailed to her first assignment in China. During her time in China, she would live out daily and sacrificially vital aspects of loving others as Jesus has loved us. We see three of these aspects in John 13.

Serve Others

(JOHN 13:1–11)

One aspect we see clearly in John 13 regarding loving others is the call to serve them (see verses 1–11). Jesus modeled service and humility by washing the disciples' feet, including Judas. This was a task reserved for Gentile servants or slaves. Warren Wiersbe says, "Jesus was the Sovereign, yet He took the place of a servant. He had all things in His hands, yet He picked up a towel. He was Lord and Master, yet He served His followers. It has been said that humility is not thinking meanly of yourself; it is simply not thinking of yourself at all."[9] Philippians 2:1–11 provides an appropriate commentary. Jesus humbled himself to serve others, even to the point of death on a cross. When it comes to this aspect of loving others, Eleanor would walk in the steps of her Master.

In the last year of her life, Dr. Chesnut treated 5,479 patients at the women's hospital in Southern China.[10] Due to her work and that of the other missionaries, converts multiplied until "by 1915 (10 years after her martyrdom) in the city of Lien-Chou there was a church with an adult membership of over 300."[11] What mindset put her here?

In 1893, she applied to the Presbyterian Foreign Mission Board in New York. She wrote, "I am willing to be sent to whatever location may be deemed fittest. . . . But being asked if I had a preference, my thoughts turned to Siam . . . I do not, however, set my heart on any one place, but rather pray that wherever it may be will be the appointed one, that what powers I possess may be used to the best advantage."[12] And, in a letter to a friend just before she left for China she wrote, "I have had developed in me a liking for medical study, although I did not seriously think of the matter until late. It seemed to me such an utter impossibility to carry out the design, as I am without means and without friends to assist. But I do trust that I am by divine appointment fitted for this work. My age—twenty-one next January. Oh! I just long to do this work."[13]

Be an Example

(JOHN 13:12–15)

Another aspect we clearly see in John 13 regarding loving others is not only to serve others but to be a *watchable and well-known example* of such service (see vv. 12–15). On this, Eleanor Chesnut was stellar in the way she followed in her Savior's footsteps. G. Thompson Brown notes, "She became well known for her travels on horseback to hold clinics in neighboring villages and for her sacrificial living in cramped and uncomfortable quarters on the second floor of the hospital."[14] In a devotion entitled "A Bathroom, a Leg and $1.50," we read about some of the sacrifices Eleanor made:

> On August 7, 1893 Eleanor was appointed a medical missionary and assigned to south China. Her work there was complicated by a poor grasp of the language and by impoverished conditions, and she continually found herself in arduous straits. On one occasion she became responsible for a demented patient who had ruined his brain with opium. "He thinks he is continually being pursued by demons," she wrote a friend. "I have no place for him but my study. He is sometimes violent and has to be carefully watched. So I am sitting here on guard now."[15]

> Her affection for the people of Lien-Chou knew no bounds. She used her bathroom as an operating room, and on one occasion used skin from her own leg as a graft for a coolie whose own leg was healing poorly following surgery.[16] She established a women's hospital in Lien-Chou, living on $1.50 a month so the rest of her salary could be used to buy bricks.[17]

In all these ways and more, Eleanor offered her life and even her health to be a living and watchable example of what it looks like to love others not merely in a generic sense, but in the way Christ loves us.

Remember Who You Are

(JOHN 13:16–17)

A third aspect of loving others the way Jesus loves us is to remember our identity. You cannot love someone in the posture of a servant if you forget you're a servant to begin with! And so John 13:16–17 reminds us on the days we are tempted to forget: we are servants of a great Master. We are messengers of a great Sovereign. We love as he loves. We serve as he serves, and we are happy to do so. We trust him as to where he sends us. We trust him as to whom he sends us.

The same day Eleanor died, the Presbyterian Foreign Missions Board received a letter from Dr. Chesnut, which she had written weeks earlier. It is her last known letter. In it she wrote a poem concerning her own questions concerning divine guidance:

> Being in doubt, I say
> Lord, make it plain!
> Which is the true, safe way?

Which would be in vain?
I am not wise to know,
Not sure of foot to go,
My blind eyes cannot see
What is so clear to Thee;
Lord, make it clear to me.
Being perplexed, I say,
Lord make it right!
Night is as day to Thee,
Darkness as light.
I am afraid to touch
Things that involve so much;
My trembling hand may shake,
My skillness hand may break—
Thine can make no mistake.[18]

Jesus served His disciples because of his humility, love, and trust in the Father—a trust so deep that even in His own dark night of the soul, as he pondered God's guidance and plan regarding his own impending death, he would say, "Father, if you are willing, take this cup away from me—nevertheless, not my will, but yours, be done" (Luke 22:42). Jesus didn't just teach a lesson in John 13 about the value of remembering one's identity in order to serve others. All four Gospels show us that he *lived* it. Even in his deepest agony and most perplexing moment, Jesus remembered who he is—and who His Father is—and banked on these truths to see him through to the other side of death. Eleanor Chesnut did the same.

Our Love for Others Will Show the Nations We Are Jesus's Disciples

(JOHN 13:35)

As we've seen so far, to love others as Jesus loves us, we must serve others, be an example, and remember who we are. And what do these three aspects of love result in? John 13:35 puts it this way: "By this all people will know that you are my disciples, if you have love for one another" (ESV).

Eleanor Chesnut loved her Savior. Because she loved him, she beautifully loved those deemed unlovable by many—often to a degree others likely considered inordinate. But as C. S. Lewis once said, "It is probably impossible to love any human being simply 'too much.' We may love him too much *in proportion* to our love for God; but it is the smallness of our love for God, not the greatness of our love for the man, that constitutes the inordinacy."[19] Immersing herself in the world of the needy, she gave no regard to social class, ethnicity, gender, or any other cultural distinction. Concerning her call to serve and minister in China she said, "I am more and more grateful for the privilege of working here in China. . . . I would be glad to devote the rest of my life to the work. . . . It would be a pleasure."[20] And the result of her deep and demonstrated love was exactly as John 13:35 would teach, namely, that it was both missiological in its reach and irrefutable to the watching world.

Our Love for Others Is Missiological

Do you see it in our text? "All people." The nations are in view here. All people will know of Jesus by how we live and love, by how we serve and die. They will know that we belong to Jesus, that we follow and trust in Jesus. Eleanor believed this with all her heart. She would say, "I don't think we are in any danger, and if we are, we might as well die suddenly in God's work as by some long, drawn out illness at home."[21]

One year she asked the board to send another physician to take her hospital at Lien-Chou. She wanted permission to move to an outlying city where no work was being done, saying that she was not afraid to live alone. But the board felt that the plan was unwise. It indicated, however, her splendid courage and zeal. During her furlough she heard Dr. Fenn of Peking in an address on China say that if he had many lives he would gladly give them all for that country. She turned to a friend and said, "I honestly believe that I could say the same."[22]

As both John 13:35 and Eleanor's life teach us, the way a Christian loves others has an undeterrable missionary impulse to it; it keeps pressing beyond the borders and into people groups others wouldn't dare tread.

Our Love for Others Is Irrefutable Evidence That We Belong to Jesus

Our text in John 13:35 says "all people" will come to know something if they look upon the love displayed by Jesus's disciples. But what is this "something" all people come to know? "That you are my disciples." Not that we're just nice people. Nor that we're somehow especially altruistic. Rather, we are known to *belong to Jesus* by the way we love others. Because only King Jesus presses his presence through to all kinds of people, through any border! While many people find it easy enough to love those who love them back (Matt. 5:46), *this* kind of love—the kind that presses toward those deemed a stranger, those who don't love us in return, or even those who would require major discomfort of us—is a risk. But it is worth it. C. S. Lewis said it like this: "To love at all is to be vulnerable. Love anything, and your heart will certainly be wrung and possibly be broken. If you want to make sure of keeping it intact, you must give your heart to no one, not even to an animal. Wrap it carefully round with hobbies and little luxuries; avoid all entanglements; lock it up safe in the casket or coffin of your selfishness. But in that casket—safe, dark, motionless, airless—it will change. It will not be broken; it will become unbreakable, impenetrable, irredeemable.[23]

Eleanor Chesnut loved like this. Willie Jordan writes,

> Dr. Eleanor Chestnut was a medical missionary to China, and her heart was almost literally implanted in those she served. Dr. Chestnut beautifully exemplified Christ-like love. A beggar came to the hospital badly burned, but there was no skin to use for a graft. The next morning the nurses learned that the operation had been performed. When they noticed that Dr. Chestnut was limping, they realized that she had surgically cut and removed a large patch of her own skin to save the victim's life. They were shocked at such a sacrifice, for they couldn't understand why she would do that for a total stranger. Later, during the Boxer rebellion, when thousands of Christian missionaries and Chinese Christians were massacred, this servant missionary showed a selflessness that profoundly impressed the Chinese people. As she was being led to prison, she saw a little boy bruised and bleeding. She broke away from her captors, and knelt down to bind up the child's wounds. A few hours later they murdered her for her faith. More than fifty years later, people in China still talked about

> the foreign doctor whose loving care for others made them think of her Jesus.[24]

Tertullian, the early church apologist, noted how the pagans of his day marveled at how Christians lived, especially when facing persecution and martyrdom. He wrote, "See how they love one another . . . how they are ready even to die for one another."[25] Such love—the kind that presses into sacrifice and, if necessary, descends even to the level of death—is irrefutable evidence that a person belongs to King Jesus. This type of love and service was seen by "all people" surrounding Eleanor Chesnut, and the same should be true of Christians today who claim the name of Christ.

Conclusion

In John 15:12–15 (ESV) Jesus said, "This is my commandment, that you love one another as I have loved you. Greater love has no one than this, that someone lay down his life for his friends. You are my friends if you do what I command you. No longer do I call you servants, for the servant does not know what his master is doing; but I have called you friends, for all that I have heard from my Father I have made known to you." He loved us. He served us. He died for us. Eleanor Chesnut paid the ultimate price as she followed in the footsteps of her Lord and King.

On October 29, 1905, at the height of anti-foreign sentiment in China, three new missionaries arrived at the Lien-Chou Hospital: a single woman, and a married couple (with their eleven-year-old daughter). Less than forty-eight hours later, a Chinese mob attacked the hospital. The little girl was stabbed to death and thrown in the river. Her parents and the single woman were clubbed to death. Eleanor might have safely escaped, but she returned to the area of danger to help her fellow missionaries. Four men from the mob flung her into the river; then, one of them speared her with a pitchfork—"once in the neck, once in the breast, and once in the lower part of the abdomen."[26] The other men jumped in the water and held Dr. Chesnut under till she drowned. She was only thirty-seven years old. One account of her martyrdom notes, "The last act of Dr. Chesnut, one of characteristic thoughtfulness and unselfishness, was to tear off a portion of her skirt and bind up an ugly gash on the head of a Chinese boy who had been accidentally struck by a stone. Her last words were a plea for Mr. and Mrs. Peale. She told the mob to kill her if they desired to do so, but to spare the new missionaries who had just arrived and who could not possibly have offended them."[27] Her words went unheeded.

Eleanor's death and the deaths of the others were reported in the *New York Times* on November 2, 1905. Reverend Arthur J. Brown summarized their lives in this way:

> All of these beloved missionaries had unreservedly consecrated themselves to the service of Christ. They were ready to go at any time that the Master called. They were faithful unto death, and they have received the martyr's crown. May God give unto us all like fidelity! In the immortal words of Lincoln at Gettysburg, "We should be dedicated to the great task remaining before us; that from these honored dead we take increased devotion to that cause for which they gave the last full measure of devotion; that we highly resolve that these dead shall not have died in vain."[28]

Back home, the story of these missionaries—particularly their courage—caused others to wish to follow in their footsteps.

The church decided to redouble their missionary efforts in Lien-Chou. Several men stepped in to take over the work. Funds were raised for the mission as a memorial to the martyrs, and in 1907 Dr. Elizabeth Carper arrived to administrate the women's hospital in Dr. Chesnut's place. In 1915, three hundred believers worshipped at the Lien-Chou church. The work went on, and we still remember the courage God gave to a little orphan girl from Waterloo, Iowa.

On the wall of one of the rooms of the Presbyterian Foreign Missions Board in New York City is a bronze memorial tablet bearing this inscription:

In Loving Memory
of the
Missionary Martyrs
Of Lien-Chou, China,
Eleanor Chestnut, M.D.
Mrs. Ella Wood Machle
And her little daughter Amy
Rev. John Rogers Peale
Mrs. Rebecca Gillespie Peale
Who, for Christ's sake, suffered cruel death at
Lien-Chou, China, October 28, 1905.
"They loved not their lives unto the death."
Rev. xii.11.
"They climbed the steep ascent of heaven
Through peril, toil, and pain;
O God, to us may grace be given
To follow in their train."

John Piper sums it up perfectly: "This is what Jesus is calling for among us. . . . Go low in foot-washing-like service to one another. Lay down your lives, your privileges, for one another.

Love your brothers and sisters across all racial and ethnic lines. Love the weakest and oldest and youngest. Love the disabled. Love the lonely trouble maker. . . . How blessed the church . . . that loves like this."[29]

3

The Lord Is My Refuge—Plainly Put on Display in the Life of Missionary

Ann Hasseltine Judson[1]

PSALM 142

Ann ("Nancy") Judson has rightly been called "the mother of modern missions."[2] This title is all the more amazing when you consider she died from cerebral meningitis at the young age of thirty-seven in the Southeast Asia country of Burma, modern-day Myanmar. Her grave, along with her little daughter Maria, is located there under what her husband Adoniram called "the hope tree." Ann did not have a long life, but it was a full life in service to King Jesus.

Psalm 142 is a psalm of lament written by David from a cave (either Adullam in 1 Sam. 22 or En-gedi in 1 Sam. 24). It could easily have been written by Ann Hasseltine Judson on numerous occasions as she served King Jesus and labored among the Burmese people for their salvation. It is a psalm filled with "great distress."[3] The honesty of the psalm in its cries for help should instruct us about the realities of forsaking everything to follow Jesus. The hope that arises even in difficult and painful circumstances should inspire us. Three movements will be noted and examined in our study of these seven verses.

God Hears the Cries of Your Heart

(PSALM 142:1–2)

The first two verses flow with words of passionate verbal petition to the Lord (*Yahweh*): "I cry;" "I plead;" "I pour out;" "I reveal." Aloud David pleads "for mercy" from the Lord. Aloud he complains and tells his troubles to the One who is his "shelter," "portion," and rescuer (vv. 5–6). This crying is not a one-time event. The crying and pleading are ongoing and continuous. Spurgeon wisely points out, "We do not show our trouble before the Lord that *he* may see it, but that *we* may see *him*. It is for *our* relief, and not for his information."[4]

Ann Judson, of all those who followed the Lord's call to the international mission field, knew we have a God who anywhere, anytime, and under any circumstances hears our prayers. She learned this truth early in her life, and it sustained her until her death. Ann was born just before Christmas in 1789 in Bradford, Massachusetts. She was the youngest of five children. She was lovely, cheerful, popular, highly intelligent, and beautiful. During her first sixteen years, she seldom felt any real conviction concerning salvation. God, however, used Hannah More's *Strictures on the Modern System of Female Education*, John Bunyan's *Pilgrim's Progress,* and a visit to an aunt to stir her heart and bring her to Christ. Her own words from her journals beautifully describe her conversion as she cried out and fled to Jesus:

> I longed for annihilation; and if I could have destroyed the existence of my soul, with as much

ease as that of my body, I should quickly have done it. But that glorious Being, who is kinder to his creatures than they are to themselves, did not leave me to remain long in this distressing state. I began to discover a beauty in the way of salvation by Christ. He appeared to be just such a Savior as I needed. I saw how God could be just, saving sinners through him. I committed my soul into his hands, and besought him to do with me what seemed good in his sight. When I was thus enabled to commit myself into the hands of Christ, my mind was relieved from that distressing weight which had borne it down for so long a time. . . . A view of his purity and holiness filled my soul with wonder and admiration. I felt a disposition to commit myself unreservedly into his hands, and leave it with him to save me or cast me off, for I felt I could not be unhappy, while allowed the privilege of contemplating and loving so glorious a Being. I now began to hope, that I had passed from death unto life. When I examined myself, I was constrained to own, that I had feelings and dispositions to which I was formerly an utter stranger. I had sweet communion with the blessed God, from day to day; my heart was drawn out in love to Christians of whatever denomination; the sacred Scriptures were sweet to my taste; and such was my thirst for religious knowledge, that I frequently spent a great part of the night in reading religious books. O how different were my views of myself and of God, from what they were, when I first began to enquire what I should do to be saved! I felt myself to be a poor lost sinner, destitute of everything to recommend myself

> to the divine favour; that I was, by nature, inclined to every evil way; and that it had been the mere sovereign, restraining mercy of God, not my own goodness, which had kept me from committing the most flagrant crimes. This view of myself humbled me in the dust, melted me into sorrow and contrition for my sins, induced me to lay my soul at the feet of Christ, and plead his merits alone, as the ground of my acceptance.[5]

In 1806, at the age of sixteen, Ann publicly confessed Christ at a revival. During the same revival, her entire family also was converted. God quickly planted a missionary heart in Ann. Somewhere around the age of nineteen, she wrote, "*March 17* [probably 1809]. Have had some enjoyment in reading the life of David Brainerd [pioneer missionary to the North American Indians]. It had a tendency to humble me, and excite desires to live as near to God, as that holy man did. Have spent this evening in prayer for quickening grace. Felt my heart enlarged to pray for spiritual blessings for myself, my friends, the church at large, the heathen world, and the African slaves. Felt a willingness to give myself away to Christ, to be disposed of as he pleases. Here I find safety and comfort. Jesus is my only refuge."[6]

By the age of twenty-one, Ann was determined to become a missionary. The same was true of a young Congregational minister named Adoniram Judson who was smitten the first time he saw Ann. On February 5, 1812, they married. Twelve days later they, along with Samuel and Harriet Newell, set sail for India on a ship called the *Caravan* as the first commissioned missionaries from America. God had heard the cries of Ann's heart in salvation and the cries of her heart to know and do his will. Again, her journals give a glimpse into God's powerful work in her heart:

August 8, 1810. Endeavoured to commit myself entirely to God, to be disposed of, according to his pleasure. . . . I do feel, that his service is my delight. Might I but be the means of converting a single soul, it would be worth spending all my days to accomplish.

September 10. For several weeks past, my mind has been greatly agitated. An opportunity has been presented to me, of spending my days among the heathen, in attempting to persuade them to receive the Gospel. Were I convinced of its being a call from God, and that it would be more pleasing to him, for me to spend my life in this way than in any other, I think I should be willing to relinquish every earthly object, and in full view of dangers and hardships, give myself up to the great work. A consideration of this subject has occasioned much self-examination, to know on what my hopes were founded, and whether my love to Jesus was sufficiently strong to induce me to forsake all for his cause.

October 28. I rejoice, that I am in his hands—that he is every where present, and can protect me in one place as well as in another. He has my heart in his hands, and when I am called to face danger, to pass through scenes of terror and distress, he can inspire me with fortitude, and enable me to trust in him, Jesus is faithful; his promises are precious. If I have been deceived in thinking it my duty to go to the heathen, I humbly pray, that I may be undeceived, and

> prevented from going. But whether I spend my days in India or America, I desire to spend them in the service of God, and be prepared to spend an eternity in his presence. O Jesus, make me live to thee, and I desire no more.
>
> *Sabbath (updated).* Blessed Jesus, I am thine forever. Do with me what thou wilt; lead me in the path in which thou wouldest have me to go, and it is enough.[7]

God Knows What You Are Going Through

(PSALM 142:3–4)

Verses 3–4 contain "the lament proper."[8] David's trials are weighing him down. Yet, even in his distress, David is confident that the Lord knows his way and that the Lord sees everything he is going through. Still, what he is experiencing is almost overwhelming.

> My spirit is weak [ESV, "faints"]. . . .
> They have hidden a trap for me. . . .
> No one stands up for me;
> there is no refuge for me;
> no one cares about me.

If we are honest, we have all been where David is. This is how we feel when times are tough and when service to Jesus is excruciatingly difficult. Again, few people who have followed in the footsteps of our Lord Jesus have known hardship better than Ann Judson. Just reflect on the following:

- On the way to India, she and her companions became convinced of believer's baptism and had to forgo all support from the Congregationalists who sent them.
- They would be denied entry into India and forced to go to Burma, which was extremely hostile to Christianity.
- Harriett Newell, Ann's dearest friend, would die in childbirth (as would the child) at the tender age of nineteen, never making it to the mission field.
- Ann's first child was stillborn.
- Her second child, a boy named Roger, died before his first birthday.
- In 1820, after six years on the field, Ann nearly died and had to go to Calcutta and eventually back to America to recover. She would be separated from her beloved husband for two years.

When Ann returned to Burma in 1824, she became pregnant. Soon thereafter, Adoniram and fellow missionary Jonathan Price were imprisoned for seventeen months. The conditions were beyond brutal. Adoniram nearly died several times and considered suicide. During this period, Ann gave birth to a baby girl named Maria, pled repeatedly for her husband's release, and daily walked two miles to supply him and others with water and food. Of this time, she would write:

> Sometimes for days and days together, I could not go into the prison, till after dark, when I had two miles to walk, in returning to the house. O how many, many times, have I returned from that dreary prison

> at nine o'clock at night, solitary and worn out with fatigue and anxiety. . . . My prevailing opinion was, that my husband would suffer violent death; and that I should, of course become a slave, and languish out a miserable though short existence in the tyrannic hands of some unfeeling monster. But the consolations of [Christ], in these trying circumstances, were neither "few nor small." It taught me to look beyond this world, to that rest, that peaceful happy rest, where Jesus reigns, and oppression never enters.[9]

During this time Ann again became seriously ill and nearly died, as did little Maria. Her own words are more than one can fathom both in her suffering but also in her faith in God's providence:

> Our dear little Maria was the greatest sufferer at this time, my illness depriving her of her usual nourishment and neither a nurse nor a drop of milk could be procured in the village. By making presents to the jailers, I obtained leave for Mr. Judson to come out of prison [in fetters] and take the little emaciated creature around the village, to beg a little nourishment from those mothers who had young children. Her cries in the night were heart-rending, when it was impossible to supply her wants. I now began to think the very afflictions of Job had come upon me. When in health I could bear the various trials and vicissitudes, through which I was called to pass. But to be confined with sickness, and unable to assist those who were so dear to me, when in distress, was almost too much for me to bear: and had it not been for the consolations of [my Lord], and an assured

> conviction that every additional trial was ordered by infinite love and mercy, I must have sunk under my accumulated suffering.[10]

God knows what we are going through. Any pain, any suffering, and any trial must first pass through the hands of an infinitely wise and loving heavenly Father.

God Will Deliver You as Your Refuge

(PSALM 142:5–7)

Despite his dire circumstances, David is confident the Lord will meet his needs. James Boice helpfully identifies four things God was to David (and for us) in verses 5–7.[11] First, God is our **refuge** (v. 5). In verse 4, as David looked around, he saw no refuge. Now, as he looks up, he sees God as his refuge. He shouts, "You are my shelter." You are "a trustworthy place of safety."[12]

Second, God is our "**portion** in the land of the living." He is our living inheritance, an inheritance far more valuable than any earthly possession. Third, he is our **Savior**. In our broken, weak, and humbled condition, those who persecute and pursue us are too strong. They are too much for us to handle. Only God can deliver us. Only he can rescue us. Only he can save us. Fourth, he is our **liberator.** He is the one who can set us free literally and figuratively from prison. In response to this truth, the psalmist says he will "praise [the Lord's] name." He continues, "The righteous will gather around me because [God deals] generously with me." Interestingly, the verb "gather" or "surround" could possibly mean, in this context, "put a crown on me."[13]

Ann Judson would experience the truth of verse 7 in an unexpected way. Adoniram would be released from prison, and he and Ann would be joyfully reunited. However, it would last for only two weeks. Adoniram would be called away on business for the Burmese government. While he was away, Ann died on October 24, 1826, from cerebral meningitis. Her body had been broken from the ordeal and sufferings of the previous two years. Tragically, little Maria would follow her mother in death to glory six months later. Concerning his loss, Adoniram would write to Ann's mother:

> The next morning we made [Maria's] last bed in the small enclosure that surrounds her mother's lonely grave. Together they rest in hope, under the hope tree, which stands at the head of the graves, and together, I trust, their spirits are rejoicing after a short separation of precisely six months. And I am left alone in the wide world. My own dear family I have buried; one in Rangoon, and two in Amhurst. What remains for me but to hold myself in readiness to follow the dear departed to that blessed world, "Where my best friends, my kindred dwell, Where God my Saviour reigns."[14]

Conclusion

It is difficult to summarize all this incredible woman accomplished in her short life. Her story and writings alone mobilized untold numbers of women to go to the nations for the cause of Christ and the Great Commission. And to this accomplishment we may add the following:

- She modeled joint ministry partnership with her husband. In a letter to her sister in 1812, she wrote, "Good female schools are extremely needed in this country. I hope no missionary will ever come out here without a wife, as she, in her sphere, can be equally useful with her husband."[15] They were truly a dynamic duo in ministry.
- She was an evangelist, taught women the gospel, adopted orphans, and started schools for children.
- She was a superb linguist and translator who learned spoken Burmese and Siamese better than her husband. She translated into Burmese tracts, a catechism, the Gospel of Matthew, and the books Daniel and Jonah.
- She wrote a history of their mission work entitled "A Particular Relation of the American Baptist Mission to the Burmese Empire" (1823). Her plan was to use the proceeds to redeem little girls sold into slavery.[16]

In an appeal to American women, "Address to Females in America, Relative to the Situation of Heathen Females in the East," she closes with these powerful words:

> Shall we, my beloved friends, suffer minds like these to lie dormant, to wither in ignorance and delusion, to grope their way to eternal ruin, without an effort on our part, to raise, to refine, to elevate, and to point to that Saviour who has died equally for them as for us? Shall we sit down in indolence and ease, indulge in all the luxuries with which we are

> surrounded, and which our country so bountifully affords, and leave beings like these, flesh and blood, intellect and feeling, like ourselves, and of *our own sex*, to perish, to sink into eternal misery? No! by all the tender feelings of which the female mind is susceptible, by all the privileges and blessings resulting from the cultivation and expansion of the human mind, by our duty to God and our fellow creatures, and by the blood and groans of him who died on Calvary, let us make a united effort; let us call on all, old and young, in the circle of our acquaintance to join us in attempting to meliorate the situation, to instruct, to enlighten and save females in the Eastern world; and though time and circumstances should prove that our united exertions have been ineffectual, we shall escape at death that bitter thought, that Burman females have been lost, without an effort of ours to prevent their ruin.[17]

Ann Judson was a remarkable woman of God. Of that there can be no doubt. May our great God multiply her kind ten thousand times over so that His name might be made famous among the nations for their eternal good and for his eternal glory.

Precious in the Sight of the Lord Is the Death of His Saints–a Powerful Truth Revealed in the All-Too-Brief Life of Missionary

Harriet Newell[1]

PSALM 116

In her book *A Path through Suffering*, Elisabeth Elliot asks, "Did the earthly life of our Lord appear to be a thundering success? Would the statistics of souls won, crowds made into faithful disciples, sermons heeded, commands obeyed, be impressive? Hardly."[2] These words not only apply to our Savior; they also apply to one of his choice servants, a precious young lady who would die at the tender age of nineteen on the way to a mission field she would never see: Harriet Atwood Newell. And like our Lord, her death would not be in vain. Rather, as was said at her memorial service, her death "will certainly turn to the advantage of missions."[3]

In so many ways the life and death of Harriet Newell is a marvelous reflection of Psalm 116, the fourth of the Egyptian Hallel psalms (Pss. 113–118). Jews sang these psalms at Passover to celebrate how the Lord rescued the Hebrews from Egyptian slavery. Our Lord would have sung this song with his disciples on the night his passion began. It is a personal psalm of gratitude and thanksgiving for the Lord's deliverance from trouble—trouble so great that it nearly led to death. Several features make this psalm appropriate for this use:

- Four times the psalmist speaks of calling on the Lord (vv. 2, 4, 13, 17).
- Three times allusions are made to death (vv. 3, 8, 15).
- Two times the author promises to fulfill his vows to the Lord "in the presence of all his people" (vv. 14, 18).
- The personal pronouns "I," "me," and "my" occur in every verse of the psalm but two (vv. 5, 19).

The psalm is deeply personal, reflecting on what God has done and continues to do for us and what is our rightful response. This biblical truth could have enabled Harriet to write in her journal at the age of eighteen—a little more than a year before she would die on the Isle of France (Mauritius)—these powerful words: "O that I had a thousand pious relatives well-calculated for the important station of missionaries. . . . I would say to them, 'Go and let the destitute millions of Asia and Africa know there is compassion in the hearts of Christians. Tell them of the love of Jesus and the road to bliss on high.'"[4]

Seven truths from this wonderful psalm are beautifully reflected in the life of Harriet Newell.

Faithful Servants Have a Passionate Love for the Lord

(PSALM 116:1)

The psalmist begins by proclaiming his love for the Lord. You can feel his emotion and excitement as he declares, "I love the Lord [*Yahweh*]." Why does he love the Lord? He loves the God who hears and answers prayers, unlike the dumb idols of Psalm 115:6 that "have ears but cannot hear."

Like the psalmist, Harriet also loved the Lord who heard her prayers. Harriet was born October 10, 1793, in Haverhill, Massachusetts. She had a deep and passionate love for her Lord. She took great delight in referring to him as her "Immanuel." This intimate love is not surprising as she lost her earthly father on May 8, 1808, when she was fourteen years old. Dying of tuberculosis, he left behind a wife and nine children. Harriet believed with the psalmist that God her Father heard her voice and pleas for mercy. A few entries from her writing exemplify her love for and prayers to her heavenly Father:

> **Praying for a lost friend:** "I have just formed a solemn resolution of devoting one part of every day to fervent cries to God for a near and dear friend. Who knows but my Father in heaven will lend a listening ear to the voice of my supplications and touch her heart with conviction and converting grace!"[5]
>
> **Confident in his discipling hand:** "I think I am willing to bear whatever God sees fit to lay upon me. Let my dear Heavenly Father inflict

> the keenest anguish, I will submit, for He is infinitely excellent, and can do nothing wrong."[6]
>
> **Captivated by his love:** "How condescending is God to permit hell-deserving sinners to commune with Him at His table! What on earth can equal the love of Jehovah! He treats those who are by nature His *enemies*, like *children*."[7]

Such love moved Harriet to love her Immanuel passionately in return.

Faithful Servants Continually Call on the Lord for Help

(PSALM 116:2–4)

Verse 2 naturally flows from verse 1 and then moves into one of the main themes of the psalm: death. Because the Lord hears our voice and cries for mercy, we can be confident we have his ear (v. 2). So we call on him as long as we live; the length of life is not specified (v. 2; cf. v. 4).

The psalmist then recalls a specific time in his life when he especially needed the Lord's help. *The Message* paraphrases it this way: "Death stared me in the face, hell was hard on my heels. Up against it, I didn't know which way to turn." So, like Jonah sinking in a sea that was about to drown him, the psalmist "called on the name of the LORD" (v. 4). Flat on his back, he could only look up! At the end of his rope, he looked to the one who held the rope and cried, "LORD, save me!"

Harriet stared death in the face more than once. In 1810, at the age of seventeen, she took fever and nearly died. Yet she called on and trusted the Lord, drawing strength from the hymn by

Isaac Watts entitled "God of My Life." Often she would repeat the verse,

> God of my life, look gently down,
> Behold the pains I feel;
> But I am dumb [silent] before Thy throne,
> Nor dare dispute Thy will.

God used this time of sickness to strengthen Harriet's faith and prepare her to answer his call to go to the nations. In a series of journal entries dating February 10–25, 1810, she would write,

> What great reason have I for thankfulness to God that I am still in the land of the living and have another opportunity of recording with my pen His tender mercy and loving kindness! . . .
>
> Jesus has undertaken to be my physician. He has graciously restored me to health . . . and brought me to resign my soul into His arms and to willingly wait the event of His Providence, whether life or death. Oh, that this sickness might be for my eternal good! . . .
>
> He has again laid His chastising rod upon me by afflicting me with sickness and pain. But "I will bear the indignation of the Lord, because I have sinned against Him." I have a renewed opportunity of examining my submission to God. And I do now, as in His presence, resolve to devote myself a living sacrifice to Him. I think I can say that afflictions are good for me. . . .
>
> But I fall infinitely short of the honor due to His glorious name. When, oh when, shall I arrive at the destined port of rest and with blood-washed millions

> who praise the Lamb of God for His redeeming love? Hasten, blessed Immanuel, that glorious period when all Thy exiled children shall arrive at their eternal home and celebrate Thy praises when time and nature fail. O for a tongue to sound aloud the honors and glories of the dear, matchless Saviour![8]

Faithful Servants Know the Character of the Lord They Serve

(PSALM 116:5–7)

Those who know God best will serve him best. A knowledge of his character and his ways promotes gratitude, and it provides a motivation to trust him and serve him in a way that comes by no other means. In verse 5 we learn three things about our Lord's character: he is gracious, righteous, and compassionate. In verse 6 we learn of his ways: "The LORD guards the inexperienced," the one who in childlike faith depends on him. Indeed when "I was helpless, . . . he saved me." In verse 7, we see our proper response: serene rest and gratitude.

Even as a tender teenage girl, Harriet Newell captured a glimpse of this important truth:

> **Nov. 20, 1810, a letter to Sarah Hills:** "I still find the promises precious and Jesus unchangeable. Though I am worthless and undeserving, yet the blessed Immanuel is lovely and worthy of the united praises of saints and angels."[9]

> **Feb. 24, 1811 (journal):** "I was remarkably favored with the presence of Immanuel. Never before did I gain such access to the mercy seat and entertain

such glorious views of the character of God and such humiliating ideas of my situation as a sinner."[10]

March 25, 1811 (journal): "God has not left Himself without witness in the earth. No—He is still manifesting the riches of His grace in bringing home his chosen ones. . . . I cannot but stand amazed to see the salvation of God! 'Come, behold the works of the Lord' [Ps. 46:8]."[11]

Faithful Servants Trust in the Lord Even in Terrible Suffering

(PSALM 116:8–11)

Those who love the Lord and serve him well are not immune from hardship and suffering. They should expect it as they walk in the footsteps of their Suffering Servant Savior. The psalmist could rejoice in God's deliverance (v. 8) and in the truth that he walks "before the LORD in the land of the living" (v. 9). But how did he get here? He had traveled a road that brought his soul to the edge of death, filled his eyes with tears, and saw his feet stumbling to maintain his walk with the Lord. It was not an easy path. Still, as verse 10 testifies, he believed even as he said, "I am severely oppressed." In contrast to the God he could trust in his suffering, he also saw another truth more clearly than ever and could shout in his alarm: "Everyone is a liar." In their depravity and sinfulness, people are perpetually unreliable. God, however, is not. People may lie, but God only tells the truth.

Perhaps no event in the life of Harriet and her husband, Samuel Newell, illustrates this truth so well as the tragic death of their newborn baby girl. She would live only five days and be buried at sea. Harriet became pregnant soon after her marriage to Samuel. Their little daughter was a honeymoon baby conceived at sea as they traveled almost eighteen thousand miles to India. Interestingly, she never once mentions her pregnancy in her letters or journal, never using the morning sickness and fatigue that hit her at sea as an excuse to complain or question God. In the last letter she would ever pen, she shared these words with her mother:

> Port Louis, Isle of France, Nov. 3, 1812. My ever dear Mother, since I wrote you last, I have been called by God to rejoice and weep, for afflictions and mercies have both alternately fallen to my lot. I address you now from a bed of great weakness—perhaps for the last time. Yes, my dear Mama, I feel this mud-walled cottage shake, and expect ere long to become an inhabitant of the world of spirits. Eternity, I feel, is just at hand. But let me give you some account of God's dealings with me, which I shall do at intervals, as strength will admit.
>
> On the cabin floor, with no other attendant but my dear husband, we could weep for joy and call ourselves the happiest of the happy. [She had just given birth to a baby girl, also named Harriet]. But alas! On the evening of the 5th day, the dear object of our love was snatched from us by death, and on the day following committed to its watery grave. Heart-rending stroke to a parental heart! Mine almost bled with deep anguish.[12]

She was never able to finish the letter.

Faithful Servants Keep Their Word and Serve the Lord out of Gratitude for Their Salvation

(PSALM 116:12–14)

One of the great dangers to those who have been saved for many years is losing the wonder of their salvation. We can take for granted what Jesus did for us on the cross, how he bore in his body the wrath of God in our place. It becomes a common thing. The psalmist was acutely aware of this danger, and he provides a helpful remedy to avoid this debilitating spiritual disease.

Never lose sight of God's benefits or his blessings (v. 12). In other words, day by day ask yourself the question, What might I do for my Lord given all He has done and will continue to do for me? Notice that word "all"! It is crucial. Reflect on past, present, and future grace. In his book *Future Grace: The Purifying Power of the Promises of God,* John Piper puts it this way:

> The gospel events of history have an ever-present impact on the believer. Romans 5:8 says it best with its verb tenses. "God *shows* [present tense] his love for us in that while we were still sinners, Christ died [past tense] for us." This means that the past gospel events mediate the present experience of the love of God. We feel loved *now* by God because of the effect of those *past* gospel events. This profound sense of being loved by God *now* is the way that past grace becomes the foundation for our faith in future grace—that God will fulfill every promise for our good.[13]

Reflecting on God's past benevolence, I will come to Him to ask and receive even more from Him! Charles Spurgeon said it like this:

> The best return for one like me,
> So wretched and so poor,
> Is from His gifts to draw a plea,
> And ask Him still for more.[14]

We avoid spiritual lethargy and complacency by asking God for more of what he has already given us, is giving us, and will give us—a "cup of salvation" full and overflowing. Jesus took the cup of God's wrath and, in its place, gives us a cup of salvation! No wonder the psalmist now, and only now, says in verse 14, "I will fulfill my vows to the LORD in the presence of all his people" (cf. v. 18). Out of hearts overflowing with gratitude, we must declare to "all his people" how great is our God. Reflecting on his benefits in saving us, we cannot keep this good news to ourselves.

How do we see this lived out in Harriet Newell? Converted at age twelve, Harriet would write, "I was brought to cast my soul on the Saviour of sinners and rely on Him alone for salvation. . . . I was filled with a sweet peace and a heavenly calmness which I never can describe. The honors, applauses, and titles of this vain world appeared like trifles light as air. The character of Jesus appeared infinitely lovely, and I could say with the psalmist, 'Whom have I in heaven but Thee, and there is none on earth I desire besides Thee!' [Ps 73:25]."[15]

The following journal entries give evidence of her growing passion to make known this salvation to all peoples:

> **July 16, 1809:** "What am I, that I should be blessed with the gospel's joyful sound, while so many are

now perishing in heathen darkness for lack of knowledge of Christ?"[16]

July 26, 1809: "But I think I could say that it was good for me to be afflicted [v. 10]. God was graciously pleased to assist me in calling upon His name, and permitted me to wrestle with Him in prayer . . . for the conversion of sinners."[17]

August 7, 1811: "Providence now gives me an opportunity to go myself to the heathen. Shall I refuse the offer? Shall I love the glittering toys of this dying world so well that I cannot relinquish them for God? Forbid it heaven! Yes, I will go. However weak and unqualified I am, there is an all-sufficient Saviour ready to support me. In God alone is my hope. I will trust His promises and consider it one of the highest privileges that could be conferred upon me to be permitted to engage in His glorious service among the wretched inhabitants of India."[18]

Faithful Servants Believe That in Life and Death They Are Valued by the Lord

(PSALM 116:15)

In Oswald Chambers's *My Utmost for His Highest*, the February 5 devotion reads,

> It is one thing to follow God's way of service if you are regarded as a hero, but quite another thing if the road marked out for you by God requires becoming a doormat under other peoples' feet. God's purpose

> may be to teach you to say, "I know how to be abased." (like Paul) Are you ready to be less than a drop in the bucket? To be so totally insignificant that no one remembers you even if they think of those you served? Are you willing to give and be poured out until you are all used up and exhausted—not seeking to be ministered to, but to minister?[19]

Verse 15 comes out of nowhere. In a psalm rejoicing in God's deliverance from death, it does not seem to fit. Yet it does. The same God who delivers us *from* death is the God who delivers us *through* death. And the death of even one of God's saints is a precious thing, a "valuable" thing, to Him. He values highly their death and sees it as a costly thing. The NLT translates verse 15, "The LORD cares deeply when his loved ones die."

It is hard for me to imagine that the death of any saint was more precious to King Jesus than that of Harriet Newell. As a teenager newly married, she left her widowed mother and eight brothers and sisters, knowing and accepting that she would never see them again. She was pregnant for most of the four-month journey to India, where she and Samuel would be denied permanent residence. On the way to the Isle of France, with only her husband at her side, she would deliver a baby girl they named Harriet, only to watch her die five days later. Less than a month later, taken with both tuberculosis and pneumonia, Harriet's mother would also die. And yet as the hour of her death approached, she could write to Ann Judson, "How dark and mysterious are the ways of Providence. . . . But 'it is well.' Everything that God does must be right, for He is a being of infinite wisdom as well as power. . . . I think I have enjoyed the light of Immanuel's countenance and have known joys too great to be expressed."[20]

In describing Harriet's death to her mother, Samuel would write,

> She was by no means alarmed at the idea of death, nor was she melancholy. She was calm, patient, and resigned. During the last week of our voyage she read through the whole book of Job, and, as she afterwards told me, she "found sweet relief from every fear in submitting to a sovereign God, and could not refrain from shedding tears of joy that God should give her such comfortable views of death and eternity." . . . The enjoyment of God was what she expected and longed to find in heaven. Her mind seemed to repose with comfort and delight on the glorious perfections of Jehovah, her covenant God. She spoke repeatedly of the pleasure she took in dwelling on the character of God. . . . When I asked her if she was not willing to live longer she replied, "Yes, if I could live better than I have ever yet done. But I have had so much experience of the wickedness of my heart that if I should recover, I should expect the remainder of my life to be much like the past, and I long to get rid of this wicked heart and go where I shall sin no more." This thought, that death would be a complete deliverance from sin, she repeated many times with great delight. . . . The day, I think, before her death, I asked her how her past life appeared to her. She replied, "Bad enough—but that only makes the grace of Christ appear the more glorious." She then repeated these favorite lines:

> "Jesus, Thy blood and righteousness
> My beauty are, my heavenly dress;
> 'Midst flaming worlds in these arrayed,
> With joy shall I lift up my head."
>
> On the Sabbath of the 29th of November, the day before her death . . . Dr. Wallich, a friend of ours from Serampore, who had lately arrived in the Isle of France, called to see us. After looking at Harriet, he took me aside and told me he thought she could not live through the next day. When I told Harriet what the doctor said, she raised both hands, clasping them with eagerness, and with an expressive smile on her countenance, exclaimed—"Oh! Blessed news!"[21]

Yes, precious in the sight of the Lord is the death of his saints!

Faithful Servants Offer a Sacrifice of Praise and Thanksgiving to the Lord for All to Hear

(PSALM 116:16–19)

Our psalm concludes with the psalmist tangibly expressing his love for the Lord (v. 1). In verse 16, he gladly identifies himself as the Lord's servant out of gratitude for the Lord's deliverance from the chains of his afflictions (v. 10). In verse 17 he will offer sacrifices and praises of thanksgiving as he again (for the fourth time) calls on the name of the Lord. In verse 18, for a second time, he pledges to publicly fulfill his vows to the Lord. Finally, in verse 19, he specifies the place of his declaration and offering as the temple courts in Jerusalem, concluding with an outburst of worship, "Praise the LORD" (NLT; CSB, "Hallelujah"). Kidner says the flame of the psalmist's love for his God, "is not withdrawn to burn alone. Placed in the *midst* [of God's people], it will kindle others, and blaze all the longer and better for it."[22]

Commenting on his wife's death to a friend in Boston, Samuel Newell wrote, "Tell [Harriet's mother] that her dear Harriet never repented of any sacrifice she had made for Christ and that on her dying bed she was 'comforted by the thought of having had it in her heart to do something for the heathen, though God had seen fit to take her away before we entered on our work.'"[23]

I cannot help but wonder if she somehow knew her sacrifice of praise and thanksgiving would resound for all to hear in her death. Her memorial preacher was right when he said,

> Henceforth, everyone who remembers Harriet Newell will remember the Foreign Mission from America. And every one who reads the history of *this* mission will be sure to read the faithful record of her exemplary life and triumphant death. . . . Her life measured by months and years was *short,* but far otherwise when measured by what she achieved. She was the happy instrument of much good to the holy kingdom of Christ. She died in a glorious cause. Nor did she pray and weep and die in vain. Other causes may miscarry, but this will certainly triumph. The LORD God of Israel has pledged His perfections for its success. The time is at hand when the various tribes of India, and all the nations and kindreds of the earth, shall fall down before the KING of ZION and submit cheerfully to His reign. A glorious work is to be done among the nations. Christ is to see the travail of His soul.[24]

Conclusion

Harriet Atwood Newell died in the arms of her missionary-husband Samuel on November 30, 1812. She was only nineteen and had been married for less than a year. He would carry her to her grave and bury her alone. On her deathbed, she pled with her husband to relay to her family a final message: "Tell them—*assure* them, that I approve on my dying bed the course I have taken. *I have never repented leaving all for Christ.*"[25]

How could Harriet die in such an attitiude? Listen well to the heart of an eighteen-year-old girl poured out to her Immanuel just eight months before her transition into heaven:

> **March 26:** The sacrifices which I have made are great indeed, but the light of Immanuel's countenance can enliven every dreary scene and make the path of duty pleasant. Should I, at some future period, be destitute of *one* sympathizing friend in a foreign, sickly clime, I shall have nothing to fear. When earthly friends forsake me, "the Lord will take me up." No anticipated trials ought to make me anxious, for I know that I can do and suffer all things "through Christ who strengthens me." In His hands I leave the direction of every event, knowing that He who is infinitely wise and good can do me no wrong.[26]

Harried was buried on the Isle of France. A marble monument would be erected over her grave with the following inscription:

> Early devoted to Christ, her heart burned for the heathen; for them, she left her kindred and her native

> land, and welcomed danger and sufferings. Of excellent understanding, rich in accomplishments and virtues, she was the delight of her friends, a crown to her husband, and an ornament to the missionary cause. Her short life was bright, her death full of glory. Her name lives and in all Christian lands is pleading with irresistible eloquence for the heathen. This humble monument to her memory is erected by the American Board of Commissioners for Foreign Missions.[27]

Biographer Jennifer Adams notes that back in America there was an explosion of little girls being named Harriet Newell in honor of this brave and godly teenage missionary.[28] At her memorial service, she was called "the first martyr to the missionary cause from the American world,"[29] and the preacher drove home the significance of her passing: "The death of Harriet, instead of overcasting our prospects, will certainly turn to the advantage of missions."[30] He was right. By 1840, many from America had visited her grave. Her memoirs, which she was burning as she was about to leave for the mission field but which were spared by her mother's request, were published and widely distributed with a new edition being printed annually for the next twenty-five years. These memoirs resulted in many conversions and people answering the call to go to the nations.

Her husband Samuel would go on to serve for seven years in a successful mission in Ceylon. On May 30, 1821, his life would end from cholera before his thirtieth birthday. Once more the truth was claimed: precious in the sight of the Lord is the death of his saints![31]

5

The Lord Is My Light and My Salvation—a Wonderful Missionary Promise That Sustained

Darlene Deibler Rose

through Many Trials and Tribulations as She Served King Jesus among the Nations[1]

PSALM 27

"Remember one thing, dear: God said He would never leave us nor forsake us." Those words were spoken on March 13, 1942, and would be the last words Darlene Deibler would ever hear from her husband Russell as they were permanently separated in Japanese prison camps during World War II. Darlene was a missionary in her early twenties. She did not even have a chance to say goodbye to him. Listen to her own words and thoughts as she honestly and hopefully reflected on that heartbreaking day:

> Everything had happened so fast and without the slightest warning. Russell had said, "He will never

> leave us nor forsake us." No? What about now, Lord? This was one of the times when I thought God had left me, that He had forsaken me. I was to discover, however, that when I took my eyes off the circumstances that were overwhelming me, over which I had no control, and looked up, my Lord was there, standing on the parapet of heaven looking down. Deep in my heart He whispered, "I'm here. Even when you don't see Me, I'm here. Never for a moment are you out of My sight."[2]

Psalm 27 was a favorite of Darlene Deibler and became increasingly so during more than four years of her imprisonment for being a Christian missionary and an American. This Davidic psalm of adoration (vv. 1–6) and lament (vv. 7–14) forms part of a trio (Pss. 26–28) that instructs us on seeking and finding the Lord, especially when "an army deploys" against us, when "war breaks out" against us (v. 3), and when "false witnesses rise up against [us], breathing violence" (v. 12).[3] Our study will follow the four movements of the psalm, a psalm that is confident: (1) the Lord saves and delivers (vv. 1–3), (2) the Lord protects and lifts up (vv. 4–6), (3) the Lord hears and guides (vv. 7–12), and (4) the Lord sustains and strengthens (vv. 13–14).[4]

We Can Be Confident the Lord Will Save and Deliver Us

(PSALM 27:1–3)

The psalm begins by exclaiming confidence in the saving power of Yahweh, "The LORD is my light and my salvation." Interestingly, the Septuagint translates the word "salvation" as

"Savior."[5] Since the Lord is *my* light and *my* salvation, "whom should I fear?" Since he is "the stronghold [refuge, strength] of my life—whom should I dread?" Verse 1 is a beautiful example of Hebrew parallelism as the second line reinforces the first. It is also a great missionary verse for those taking the gospel of Jesus Christ into difficult and dangerous places of the world where opposition is intense and even life-threatening.

It is significant that the Lord is our "light." Light appears at the beginning and the end of the Bible (Gen. 1:3–4; Rev. 22:5). Its source is God, and it overcomes and defeats darkness (John 1:4–5). It is the source of life and allows people to see. It is also a symbol of purity, holiness, goodness, and blessing. It finds its grand fulfillment in a person, the Lord Jesus, who said, "I am the Light of the World" (John 8:12).

In verses 2–3 David speaks of evildoers, enemies, foes, and an army that deploy against him to devour his flesh and who break out against him with war. There is no escape. Yet he can say at the end of verse 3, "I will still be confident." Why? Verse 2 provides the answer: "My foes and my enemies stumbled and fell." His enemies will be defeated by his God. The Lord who is his light and Savior takes them down. They may try to overcome him, they may surround and enclose him, but his God can handle them all!

Darlene Deibler found all this to be true. Darlene Mae McIntosh was born on May 17, 1917. Her father was not physically well; her mother was a hardworking lady. At the age of nine, she put her trust in the Lord Jesus Christ as her light and salvation. One year later, at the age of ten, during a revival service, she sensed God's calling to give her life to missions.[6] On that night she promised Jesus, "Lord, I will go anywhere with You, no matter what it cost."[7] How could that little girl know what the Savior had planned for her?

Darlene would marry a pioneer missionary in Southeast Asia named Russell Deibler on August 18, 1937. She was only twenty years old; he was twelve years her senior. Later she would write, "My ignorance of the future held no cause for anxiety, for my spirit witnessed within me that God was and would be in control."[8]

After six months of church meetings in North America and six months of language study in Holland, the Deiblers eagerly returned to Russell's pioneer missionary work in the interior of New Guinea. Darlene accompanied Russell into the jungle to establish a new mission station near a previously unevangelized tribe that had been discovered just a few years earlier. Darlene, the first white woman any of them had ever seen, grew to deeply love these primitive people she was ministering to for King Jesus.

World War II broke out in that part of the world in 1941 and engulfed the missionaries in January 1942. The Deiblers had served in New Guinea for three years. Though they could have left and returned safely home, they and many others chose to stay. Ten Christian Missionary Alliance (CMA) missionaries and one child would die in captivity during the war because the Japanese soon took control of the area and put them under house arrest. Later they herded all foreigners into prisoner-of-war camps, placing the men in one location and the women and children in another. Darlene had pledged as a ten-year-old that she would follow Jesus anywhere regardless of the cost. She could have never imagined what that meant. "Anywhere" would cost her unbelievable suffering. Over four years Darlene would endure separation from her husband, widowhood and the brutal conditions of a WWII Japanese internment camp. She would experience near starvation, forced labor, inhumane conditions, false accusations of espionage, many serious illnesses, solitary confinement, and torture. Through it all, God sustained Darlene. He never left her nor forsook her, just as he had promised. He remained her light and salvation. In time, he would cause her adversaries to stumble and fall.

We Can Be Confident the Lord Will Protect and Lift Us Up

(PSALM 27:4–6)

David now expresses the soul's desire of all who have experienced the Lord's strength and His salvation. He says, "I have asked one thing from the LORD; it is what I desire" (v. 4). And what is that "one thing"? "To dwell in the house of the LORD all the days of [his] life, gazing on the beauty of the LORD." This beauty, he says, is found in "the house of the LORD" (v. 4), "his shelter" (v. 5), and "his tent" or tabernacle or temple (vv. 5–6). It is found in his presence, wherever that might be.

"The temple was the visible expression of the Lord's presence."[9] The one thing that matters most is to be in the presence of the Lord, beholding his beauty and pursuing him with one's whole heart. Jeremiah 29:13 promises, "You will seek me and find me when you search for me with all your heart." To see his beauty is to see his glory, know his love, and enjoy his presence as Father, Savior, Protector, and Sustainer. David saw this protection as he depended on the Lord to "conceal" him in his shelter "in the day of adversity" (ESV, "trouble"), to "hide" him under the "cover of his tent," and to set him high on a rock of safety and security (v. 5). David saw this sustaining power as the Lord lifted his head up above his enemies (v. 6). The only proper response to this great God is worship! That's why David says, "I will offer sacrifices in his tent with shouts of joy. I will sing and make music to the LORD."

To sacrifice, shout, sing, and rejoice in the Lord is easy when everything is going well. It is something else when your heart is broken and God seems silent and distant. Nothing illustrates this like the day, when at the tender age of twenty-seven, this faithful missionary received news of her husband's death. On a Sunday evening in November 1944, Darlene was informed that Russell had died after having been critically ill for some time. He had been dead for months by the time the news reached her. She writes, "I was stunned—Russell is dead. He'd been dead three months already! It was one of those moments when I felt that the Lord had left me; He had forsaken me. My whole world fell apart. . . . In my anguish of soul, I looked up. My Lord was there, and I cried out, 'But God . . . !'"[10] Immediately he answered, "My child, did I not say that when thou passest through the waters I would be with thee, and through the floods, they would not overflow thee?"[11]

Prayer, memorized Scripture, and song would be a three-cord spiritual rope that held Darlene during those terrible days. She writes,

> Much time was passed repeating Scripture. Starting with [the letter] *A*, I would repeat a verse that began with that letter, then on through the rest of the alphabet. I discovered that most of the songs we had sung when I was a little girl were still hidden in my heart, though I hadn't consciously memorized many of them.
>
> As a child and young person I had had a driving compulsion to memorize the written Word. In the cell I was grateful now for those days in Vacation Bible School, when I had memorized many single verses, complete chapters, and Psalms, as well as whole books

> of the Bible. In the years that followed I reviewed the Scriptures often. The Lord fed me with the Living Bread that had been stored against the day when fresh supply was cut off by the loss of my Bible. He brought daily comfort and encouragement—yes, and joy—to my heart through the knowledge of the Word.[12]

God has often used that same trio of encouragers for those who have suffered in a similar fashion to Darlene. However, in the midst of her sorrow, on that day, something truly remarkable and providential occurred, the full outcome of which would not be known for many years.

As the news of Russell's death spread throughout the camp, Darlene was summoned to Mr. Yamaji's office; he was the prison camp commander. He was a hard and brutal man who had beaten a male POW to death in another camp. He was standing behind the desk, and the following conversation took place:

> "Njonja Deibler, I want to talk with you," he began. "This is war."
>
> "Yes, Mr. Yamaji, I understand that."
>
> "What you heard today, women in Japan have heard."
>
> "Yes, sir, I understand that, too."
>
> "You are very young. Someday the war will be over and you can go back to America. You can go dancing, go to the theater, marry again, and forget these awful days. You have been a great help to the other women in the camp. I ask of you, don't lose your smile."
>
> "Mr. Yamaji, may I have permission to talk to you?" He nodded, sat down, then motioned for me to take the other chair.

> "Mr. Yamaji, I don't sorrow like people who have no hope. I want to tell you about Someone of Whom you may never had heard. I learned about Him when I was a girl in Sunday School back in Boone, Iowa, in America. His name is Jesus. He's the Son of Almighty God, the Creator of heaven and earth." God opened the most wonderful opportunity to lay the plan of salvation before the Japanese camp commander. Tears started to course down his cheeks. "He died for you, Mr. Yamaji, and He puts love in our hearts—even for those who are our enemies. That's why I don't hate you, Mr. Yamaji. Maybe God brought me to this place and time to tell you He loves you."[13]

Mr. Yamaji uncharacteristically jumped from his chair and left the room in tears. Darlene respectfully waited, and then quietly left when she realized he would not return to the room. The God who saves and delivers, who protects and lifts up had proven himself present. He was working, as we will see before we are finished.

We Can Be Confident the Lord Will Hear and Guide Us

(PSALM 27:7–12)

Verse 7 changes mood significantly. Some have speculated that we have two psalms joined together (vv. 1–6 and vv. 7–14). However, there is literary and rhetorical evidence that supports the original unity of the psalm. In a sense verses 7–14 provide the context from which verses 1–6 arose. Our God is a promise-keeping God, and we can rejoice and rest in that. David highlights several areas where we can count on the Lord to keep his word.

The voice that shouts and sings to him in worship (v. 6) can be confident that the Lord will hear that same voice when it prays (v. 7). A merciful and gracious answer can be our confident expectation.

Speaking to the Lord means seeking the Lord. What David does in verse 4, he is instructed to do in verse 8. And his response is what ours should be: obedient and immediate. "LORD, I will seek your face." Four negative requests in verse 9 complement David's petition: (1) "Do not hide your face from me." (2) "Do not turn your servant away in anger." (3) "Do not leave me." (4) "[Do not] abandon me." These requests also contain words of hope and confidence. David says, "You have been my helper" and you are the "God of my salvation" (v. 9). His parents might abandon him (in death or desertion), but the Lord will extend adoptive parental love and care. "The LORD cares for me" (v. 10). This care, David says, is enough.

Psalm 119:105 teaches us, "Your word is a lamp for my feet and a light on my path." We need the light of God when we face difficult and trying times. We must not rely on our emotions or feelings. We dare not trust our heart or experiences. We must stand firmly on Christ our Rock and the rock-solid direction of His Word.

David asks the Lord to "show me your way" (v. 11). He wants to live and respond to whatever he may face as the Lord would. David also asked the Lord to guide his life sovereignly, providentially, precisely, and specifically. "Lead me on a level [NIV, "straight"] path" "because of my adversaries," my enemies (v. 11). "Do not give me over to the will [NIV, NASB, "desire"; NLT, "their hands"] of my foes." Why? "For false witnesses [liars] rise up against me, breathing violence." They would do him harm. Eugene Peterson in *The Message* paraphrases it this way: "Show my enemies whose side you're on. Don't throw me to the dogs, those liars who are out to get me, filling the air with their threats."

On May 12, 1944, the Kempeitai, the Japanese secret police, came for Darlene. They falsely accused her of being a spy. The Kempeitai took her to a maximum-security prison where they kept her in solitary confinement. They took her Bible away from her. Over the door of her cell, in Indonesian, were the words, "This person must die." After the guard unlocked the door and shoved her inside, she knew she was on death row. She was imprisoned to face trial and the sentence of death. She sank to the floor. Never had she known such terror. She prayed, "O God, whatever You do, make me a good soldier for Jesus Christ."[14] But suddenly she found herself singing a song she had learned as a little girl in Sunday School:

> Fear Not, little flock, whatever your lot,
> He enters all rooms "the doors being shut."
> He never forsakes, He never is gone,
> So count on His presence in darkness and dawn.
> Only believe, only believe;
> All things are possible, only believe.[15]

She would later write, "So tenderly my Lord wrapped His strong arms of quietness and calm about me. I knew they could lock me in, but they couldn't lock my wonderful Lord out. Jesus was there in the cell with me."[16]

She was kept for weeks in a cell about six square feet and had only small amounts of rice to eat each day. She spent a great deal of time killing mosquitoes, saying, "I was tortured by hordes of them at night. They clung to the wall, too full of my good red blood to do anything else."[17] Frequently she would be taken to an interrogation room where two Japanese officers, whom she dubbed "the Brain" and "the Interrogator," would accuse her of spying, of having a radio, of getting messages to the Americans, and of knowing Morse code. They claimed to have proof of her treachery. All this she would deny. But in the process they would strike her at the base of her neck or on her forehead above her nose. There were times she thought they had broken her neck. She walked around often with two black eyes. Her beautiful black hair turned gray and white. "Bloodied but unbowed," she never wept in front of them.[18] But when she was back in her cell, she would weep and pour out her heart to the Lord. When she finished, she would hear Him whisper, "But my child, my grace is sufficient for thee. Not *was or shall be*, but it *is* sufficient." "Oh, the eternal, ever-present, undiminished supply of God's glorious grace!"[19]

The Kempeitai did not believe anything Darlene said. They informed her they had sufficient proof of her involvement in espionage—she knew she would be condemned without formal trial and be beheaded as an American spy. However, in her autobiography she writes of one of the ways the Lord had prepared her for the ordeal she now faced:

> Just two weeks before I was brought to this prison, the Lord had laid it on my heart to memorize a poem by Annie Johnson Flint. Now I knew why. After drying the tears from my face and mopping the tears from the floor with my skirt, I would sit up and sing:
>
> > He giveth more grace when the burdens grow greater.
> > He sendeth more strength when the labors increase.
> > To added afflictions He addeth His mercy,
> > To multiplied trials, His multiplied peace.

> When we have exhausted our store of endurance,
> And our strength has failed ere the day is half done,
> When we reach the end of our hoarded resources,
> The Father's full giving is only begun.
>
> His love has no limits, His grace has no measure.
> His power no boundary known unto men.
> For out of His infinite riches in Jesus,
> He giveth, and giveth, and giveth again.[20]
>
> Strength came, and I knew I could go through another interrogation, and another, and another. I was physically weak, and desperately frightened, but God gave me the courage to deport myself like a good soldier for my Lord before those cruel men.[21]

One day Darlene pulled herself up to the window of her cell and began watching some women who were in the courtyard. One woman's actions intrigued her. The woman inched toward a fence covered with vines. When she was close enough and the guard wasn't looking, a hand clutching a small bunch of bananas thrust through the vines; the woman grabbed the bananas, folded them into her clothes and walked calmly back to another group of women. After that,

> Darlene began to crave bananas. She got down on her knees and said, "Lord, I'm not asking You for a whole bunch like that woman has. I just want one banana." She looked up and pleaded, "Lord, just *one* banana."

Then she began to think—how could God possibly get a banana to her? There was really no way it could happen. She couldn't ask anyone to do it. It was impossible for her to get a banana. She prayed again, "Lord, there's no one here who could get a banana to me. There's no way for You to do it. Please don't think I'm not thankful for the rice porridge [her daily ration had changed because she suffered from dysentery and could not handle rice.] It's just that—well, those bananas looked so delicious!"

The morning after she saw the bananas she had a surprise visitor—Mr. Yamaji. [He had warmed toward her following her husband's death]. When her door was opened and she saw Mr. Yamaji's smiling face she clapped her hands and exclaimed, "Mr. Yamaji, it's just like seeing an old friend!" Tears filled his eyes and he didn't say a word but walked back into the courtyard and talked to the officers for a long time.

When he returned Mr. Yamaji was sympathetic. "You're very ill, aren't you?"

"Yes, Sir, Mr. Yamaji, I am."

"I'm going back to the camp now. Have you any word for the women?"

The Lord gave her the confidence to answer, "Yes, Sir, when you go back, please tell them for me that I'm all right. I'm still trusting the Lord. They'll understand what I mean, and I believe you do."

"All right," he replied, and turning he left.

When Mr. Yamaji and the other officers left Darlene realized she had not bowed to the men! "Oh Lord, they'll come back and beat me," she thought. When she heard the guard coming back she knew

> he was coming for her. She struggled to her feet and stood ready to go to the interrogation room. The guard opened the door, walked in and with a sweep of his hand laid at her feet—bananas! "They're yours," he said, "and they're all from Mr. Yamaji." Darlene was stunned as she counted—there were ninety-two bananas!
>
> In all my spiritual experience she said, I've never known such shame before my Lord. I pushed the bananas into a corner and wept before Him. "Lord, please forgive me; I'm so ashamed. I couldn't trust You enough to get even one banana for me. Just look at them—there are almost a hundred."
>
> In the quiet of the shadowed cell, He answered back within my heart: "That's what I delight to do, the exceeding abundant above anything you ask or think." I knew in those moments that nothing is impossible to my God.[22]

Time and time again God showed himself to be powerful and faithful to Darlene. Shortly after this, she was moments from being beheaded as a spy only to be taken from the Kempeitai back to the prison camp in Kampili. The Lord again had heard her prayers and lead her to a "level path" against her enemies.

We Can Be Confident the Lord Will Sustain and Strengthen Us

(PSALM 27:13–14)

This psalm concludes on a high note of confidence and assurance, even triumphant and victorious. Because of the power and might of the God who is our light and salvation, we can trust and rest in the Lord no matter what may come.

Verse 13 reads, "I am certain that I will see the LORD's goodness in the land of the living." How awesome it is that we can pray these words in full confidence, absolute faith, and complete certainty. The greater Son of David, the Lord Jesus, prayed such a prayer on the cross as his enemies surrounded him (v. 3), slandered him (v. 12), and violently took his life (v. 12). He commended his life, his destiny, into the hands of a heavenly Father. He knew with full confidence that he would see the goodness of the Lord three days later in the land of the living through glorious and powerful resurrection. In faith, he waited on the Lord (v. 14). He was strong in the Lord (v. 14). His heart took courage (v. 14), trusting in the perfect and sovereign plan of a good and gracious and great heavenly Father.

The God who sustained and strengthened Jesus and David will sustain you and me. He certainly sustained and strengthened the wonderful missionary Darlene Deibler Rose throughout her life.

God sustained and strengthened her in her salvation at nine years of age.

God sustained and strengthened her call to be a missionary at the age of ten—yes, ten!

God sustained and strengthened her as a young bride at age twenty.

God sustained and strengthened her when she headed to the jungles of New Guinea at twenty-one!

God sustained and strengthened her when placed under house arrest by the Japanese when she was twenty-five.

God sustained and strengthened her when she and her husband Russell were separated into different prison camps in 1942, never to see each other again in this life.

God sustained and strengthened her as she ate rats, tadpoles, dogs, runny oatmeal, maggots, and other unimaginable foods.

God sustained and strengthened her as she and others were forced to present sixty thousand dead flies a day to Mr. Yamaji because they bothered the pigs they tended, pigs who were treated better than the POWs.

God sustained and strengthened her through dengue fever, beriberi, malaria, cerebral malaria,[23] dysentery, beatings and torture, attacks of rabid dogs, false charges of espionage, the promise of beheading, solitary confinement, Allied bombings, and many other inhumane abuses.

God sustained and strengthened her when she was told of the death of beloved husband Russell and his own tortures and sufferings.

God sustained and strengthened her when she and the other POWs were finally released and she was allowed to visit the grave of her husband. She weighed all of eighty pounds.

God sustained and strengthened her when he brought her home to America and kept the fire of missions burning in her heart.

God sustained and strengthened her when he brought another missionary into her life, Gerald Rose, whom she would marry (1948) and then return with him to New Guinea in 1949.

God sustained and strengthened her as she labored on the mission field of Papua, New Guinea and the Outback of Australia for over forty years evangelizing, teaching, building landing strips, delivering babies, facing down headhunters, and loving them to Jesus.

No wonder she could write, "The twenty-seventh Psalm was a great comfort to me. . . . I knew that without God, without that consciousness of His presence in every troubled hour, I could never have made it."[24]

Conclusion

On February 24, 2004, Darlene Deibler Rose quietly passed away and entered into the presence of the King she so dearly loved and faithfully served. She was eighty-six years old. According to her obituary in the Chattanooga, Tennessee, newspaper, "Together, Darlene and Jerry were used of God to bring hundreds of Aborigines to the Lord and disciple them to Christ. They were also instrumental in beginning several indigenous churches that are pastored by natives."[25]

One person came to Christ through her faithful witness who particularly stands out as a testimony to the mysterious plans and providences of God. Following the end of World War II, Mr. Yamaji, the prison camp commander where Darlene was imprisoned, was tried and sentenced to be executed for the brutal beating to death of a man while he was in another POW camp at Pare Pare. His sentence was later commuted to life imprisonment with hard labor. Later that sentence was also commuted, and he was released. Many years later, in 1976, Darlene would learn from a friend that Mr. Yamaji had been heard on Japanese radio. He was heard sharing the gospel of Jesus Christ with the Japanese people, testifying to his cruelty in World War II but also bearing witness that he was now a different man because of Christ.[26] It was Darlene who had first told Mr. Yamaji of the gospel, and she did so on the day she learned of her husband's death.

Throughout her life, when sharing her story, Darlene would say, "I would do it all again for my Savior." No doubt many in New Guinea are grateful for her devotion. No doubt, Mr. Yamaji is grateful too! You never know what the Lord who is our light and Savior is going to do when we say and obey, "Lord, I'll go anywhere with You, no matter what it cost."[27] He will be with you as Psalm 27 promises. Are you willing to go?

6

Finding Contentment in Christ—the Life and Missionary Ministry of

Betsey Stockton,

the First Unmarried Woman to Go to the Nations

1 CORINTHIANS 7:17–24

If I was to use a baseball metaphor, Betsey Stockton (c. 1798–1865) began life with three strikes and a broken bat. She was a woman. She was black. She was born a slave. She had no idea who her father was, and she was taken away from her mother at a tender age. Oh, but what a life her heavenly Father had planned for His precious daughter. She would be converted to Christ in 1816, freed by her owner Ashbel Green, and leave America for the mission field in 1822 as the first unmarried woman to go to the nations! And her God had more in store for this remarkable woman. He would use this content and kingdom-minded servant of King Jesus to do amazing things in families and schools at home and in the nations.

What a difference a relationship with Jesus makes. Our life gains purpose and direction. Paul teaches us that because we are in Christ, we should not be anxious about anything (Phil. 4:6). Our Lord enables us to be content in whatever circumstances we find ourselves (Phil. 4:11). In 1 Corinthians 7, Paul says not to worry whether you are married, single, divorced, or widowed. Don't concern yourself about ethnic or social distinctions and status. Find contentment in your identity in Christ and your station in life, whatever it is. After all, your Lord put you where you are. Just ask Betsey Stockton.

In 1 Corinthians 7, the word "call" dominates verses 17–24. It occurs eight times in our English text and nine times in the Greek. It is correctly translated as "situation" or "condition" (ESV) in verse 20. Paul will use the word primarily to speak of the Christian's call to salvation and identity in Christ. But he will also use it to speak of our vocation, condition, or situation in life. A former slave, a single Black woman, who would be the first single woman to leave America as a missionary, exemplifies the beauty of this text better than anyone I know. Our Lord has sovereignly determined both kinds of callings. You can rest in that.

Be Content in Your Assignment from the Lord

(1 CORINTHIANS 7:17)

Paul addresses basic principles that should undergird all our thinking. God knows where you are, and he has placed you where you are. Paul lays down a principle from the Lord and his common practice (his rule or command) in all the churches: "Let each one live his life in the situation the Lord assigned when God called him" (v. 17). God has an individual plan and purpose for every one of his children. Trust in this. Be at peace in this. When God called you to salvation through his Son, he already had a course for your life mapped out. Growing out of your call to salvation is a definite calling for life sovereignly determined by God.

Paul tells the Corinthians this is not a word just for them. This is his "command" (CSB) or "rule" (ESV) for everyone "in all the churches." It is a universal command for all Christians at all times and in all circumstances. Service to God can take place in a variety of relationships and vocations within his moral will. Some specifics will no doubt change. But that is not something to fret over or worry about. John Piper is right: "Make obedience a big deal; make the *whole* aim of your life to obey the moral will of God. . . . You can have fulfillment in Christ whatever your job is."[1] If we want to see how we can make the whole aim of our life to please God, no matter the circumstances, we do not have to look any further than Betsey Stockton.

Betsey was born in the world of American chattel slavery. She was a feisty young girl by all accounts. Ashbel Green, a Presbyterian minister who would become president of Princeton University and Betsey's owner, said, "Betsey gave no evidence of piety, or any permanent seriousness, till she was twenty years old. On the contrary she was, at least until the age of thirteen or fourteen, wild and thoughtless, if not vicious."[2] However, Betsey Stockton's conversion resulted in a radical change that immediately planted in her heart a desire for the unthinkable and virtually impossible for a person of her station: the desire to be an international missionary. Eileen Moffett, a missionary in Korea from 1956 to 1981, said of Betsey, "[Her] maturing Christian faith gradually gave form in her mind a sense of the duty that Christians bear toward the 'lost' of the world . . . the conviction that salvation is found only in Christ. Betsey believed with all her heart that it is the sacred duty of Christians to offer themselves in humble obedience to God's call to carry out his plan of salvation through Jesus Christ for the world."[3]

And it is worth noting that though "some of her friends opposed her plan [to go to Africa as a missionary], she continued to read and study, hoping for such an opportunity."[4] Betsey Stockton found contentment and delight in the assignment God had for her. And she dreamed that assignment might include missions!

Be Content in Your Conditions in the Lord

(1 CORINTHIANS 7:18–22)

Paul illustrates in verses 18–22 the point he made in verse 17. The first illustration deals with religious distinctions (circumcision), and the second addresses social distinctions (slavery). These were perhaps the major or "chief" social distinctions of the day.[5] Paul addresses the issues in a question-and-answer format. Question: "Was anyone already circumcised when he was called [to Christ and salvation]?" Answer: "He should not undo his circumcision." According to Gardner, "such actions to cover a person's Jewishness appears to have taken place from time to time."[6] And the reverse situation is true as well. Question: "Was anyone called while uncircumcised?" Answer: "He should not get circumcised" (v. 18). Why? Verse 19 provides the answer: "Circumcision does not matter and uncircumcision does not matter." So, what matters? "Keeping God's commands is what matters." Galatians 6:15 provides a valuable commentary on Paul's point: "For both circumcision and uncircumcision mean nothing; what matters instead is a new creation" (cf. 2 Cor. 5:17). Being in Christ changes everything! Outward ethnic and social distinctions no longer matter as they once did. They are not unimportant, and they do not simply disappear after coming to Christ, but they no longer have priority or carry the weight they previously carried.

For a second time in verses 17–24 Paul reiterates the main point of the passage (cf. v. 17), "Let each of you remain in the situation [lit. "in the calling"] in which he was called" (v. 20). God has specifically and uniquely called you to this "situation" or "condition" (ESV). It is not accidental, nor is it fate. Reaffirming this cardinal principle, Paul makes a second application. This time he applies it to slavery. Slavery is a horrible evil in whatever time or form. In the Graeco-Roman world it was widespread. Unlike the trans-Atlantic slave trade commerce that will always be a stain on America's past, Graeco-Roman slavery was not race-based. Further, its manifestations and practice were diverse. Schreiner points out,

> One could be born a slave, sell oneself into slavery to pay debts, be sold into slavery or become a slave by being captured in war. Many slaves lived miserably, particularly those that served in the mines. Other slaves served as doctors, teachers, managers, musicians, artisans, barbers, cooks or shopkeepers, and could even own other slaves. In some instances, slaves were better educated than their masters. . . . Slaves in the Graeco-Roman world were under the control of their masters and had no independent existence. They had no legal rights, and they could suffer brutal mistreatment at the hands of their owners: masters could beat them, brand them and abuse them physically and sexually. Children born in slavery belonged to masters rather than to the parents who gave them birth. Seneca's observation exposes the evil of slavery: "You may take (a slave) in chains and at your pleasure expose him to every test of endurance; but too great violence in the striker has often dislocated a joint, or

> left a sinew fastened in the very teeth it has broken. Anger has left many a man crippled, many disabled, even when it found its victim submissive."[7]

It also should be noted that the slavery of pre-Civil War America most readily corresponds to what we read in Exodus 21:16 and 1 Timothy 1:10 ("slave traders"), which the Bible resoundingly condemns.

Paul returns to his Q&A format in verse 21. Question: "Were you called while a slave?" Answer: "Don't let it concern you." Don't allow this to control or consume you. Christ is now your all-consuming passion. He is your everything! How Christ sees you is what ultimately matters. However, Paul adds a qualification. "But if you can become free, by all means take the opportunity." This admonition to pursue freedom if the possibility presents itself finds indirect support in the book of Philemon. It also has Old Testament warrant. Schreiner notes, "The admonition, 'do not become slaves of human beings' (7:23), supports the idea that remaining as a slave is not the ideal . . . [and] this reading fits with the Old Testament, where enslaving a fellow-Hebrew is frowned upon (Exod. 21:2–11; Neh. 5:5)."[8]

Paul drives home his argument with a foundational theological truth in verse 22. "For he who is called by the Lord as a slave is the Lord's freedman. Likewise, he who is called as a free man is Christ's slave." Paul will apply this principle in 9:19–23 to the work of evangelism. Here the point is we are free from sin but slaves to Christ in our spiritual status before God. Leon Morris provides helpful commentary on Paul's "paradoxical language" in this verse. He writes:

> The slave who is called has entered the glorious liberty of the children of God. He has been freed from slavery to sin and this divine liberty matters so

> much more than his outward circumstances that he should see himself as the Lord's freedman. . . . With this goes the complementary truth that he who is a free man when called is Christ's slave. Once more the point is that outward circumstances matter little. The important thing for the free man is his relationship to Christ; his whole life is to be lived in lowly service to his Master. Nothing matters alongside this.[9]

Betsey Stockton was born into slavery to Robert Stockton of Princeton. She would be given to Stockton's daughter Elizabeth and her husband, Ashbel Green. This was providential. This brilliant little girl learned to read, encouraged by the Green family. Further, Ashbel Green was an abolitionist who gave Betsey her freedom when she was twenty. In his letter of commendation to the ABCFM, he wrote, "By me and by my wife she was never intended to be held as a slave."[10] At this point it is important to note the extraordinary gifts God gave Betsey Stockton and the transformation following her conversion. In his letter of commendation, Ashbel Green provides the best summation from historical records.

> Betsey is now about 25 years of age, has never been married. Her health, till some time after she returned to live with me in 1816, was remarkably firm and vigorous. Since that, it has been several times interrupted and is habitually delicate; but I think is improving. I have paid her full wages [as] a hired girl, for two or three years past; her services have been so valuable that I shall regret to lose them. But she had been, for a good while, exceedingly desirous to go on a mission and I am willing that she should. I

> think her, in many respects, well qualified for this. I hope she is fervently pious. There is no kind of work in a family for which she is not very expert. But I think her well qualified for higher employment in a mission than domestick [sic] drudgery. She reads extremely well; few of her age and sex have read more books on religion than she; or can give a better account of them. She has no small share of miscellaneous reading, and has a real taste for literature. She understands Geography and English grammar, pretty well. She composes her English [in] a manner that is very uncommon for one of her standing in society. She is tolerably skilled in arithmetic. She has made all of these attainments by improving her time and privileges in my family, without ever going to school at all. She calls herself Betsey Stockton. Princeton, September 3rd, 1821 Ashbel Green.[11]

In the historical context of the day, this is a remarkable witness to Betsey Stockton's character, gifts, and respect that she had among those who knew her. Once a slave, now a free woman and a missionary candidate. Betsey's conditions never deterred or stopped her from serving her Savior. God was in complete control of her life. Of this she had no doubt!

Be Content in Your Relationship with the Lord

(1 CORINTHIANS 7:23–24)

Paul builds on his argument by quoting 1 Corinthians 6:20. "You were bought at a price," the shed blood of the Son of God. In

6:19–20, the atonement of Christ sets us free from sexual immorality as we become the "temple of the Holy Spirit." Here we are set free from slavery to sin and earthly distinctions as we become slaves of Christ. Therefore, "do not become slaves of people" (v. 23). Your social status according to human standards now means nothing. As a new creation in Christ, don't be enslaved to shame as a slave or enslaved to pride as a freedman. Don't be enslaved to the opinions of men. Christ is Lord, and who he says you are counts most! Find your identity, value, and worth in Jesus!

For the third time (vv. 17, 20) Paul inserts the key that unlocks his argument. "Brothers and sisters, each person is to remain with God in the situation [ESV, "condition"] in which he was called" (v. 24). Warren Wiersbe is right: "We are prone to think that a change in circumstances is always the answer to a problem. But the problem is usually *within* us and not *around* us. The heart of every problem is the problem in the heart."[12] So, whose opinion matters most to you? Is it yours, others, or God's? He made you. He saved you. He placed you where you are. So rest in that. Join with Paul and confess with the apostle the words of Philippians 4:11–13, "I don't say this out of need, for I have learned to be content in whatever circumstances I find myself. I know both how to make do with little, and I know how to make do with a lot. In any and all circumstances I have learned the secret of being content—whether well fed or hungry, whether in abundance or in need. I am able to do all things through him who strengthens me."

Eileen Moffett and John Andrews III write of Betsey Stockton that her Christian worldview "was grounded on the premise of the love of God in Jesus Christ for the whole world—and the conviction that salvation is found only in Christ. Betsey believed with all her heart that it is the sacred duty of Christians to offer themselves in humble obedience to God's call to carry out His plan of salvation through Jesus Christ for the world. This persuasion soon blossomed into a desire to go to Africa as a missionary."[13]

Betsey received stellar recommendations as she applied for foreign missions from Ashbel Green and a friend from Princeton Theological Seminary named Michael Osborn. Osborn wrote concerning her excellent qualifications:

> I think her pious, intelligent, industrious, skillful in the management of domestic affairs, apt to teach, and endowed with a large portion of the active, preserving, self-sacrificing, spirit of a missionary. From my first acquaintance with her she has expressed a decided wish to go to the heathen. Africa was the place of her choice. The opposition of her friends has kept her until now. For about a year and a half she has been a member of my class in the Sabbath School at this place. Her recitations have been chiefly from the *S[acred] Scriptures, the Larger Catechism, Jewish Antiquities* and *Sacred Geography.* She has a larger acquaintance with sacred history and the Mosaic Institutions than almost any ordinary person, young or old, I have ever known. (By *ordinary person* you will understand me to mean such as are not clergymen or candidates for the ministry). I recollected a multitude of instances where, for my own information, I have questioned her about some fact in Biblical history, or some minute point in Jewish Antiquities, and have immediately received a correct answer. . . . I am of the opinion that few pious young ladies of her age will be found to equal her knowledge of the Bible and general theology.[14]

Betsey Stockton was appointed as a missionary by the ABCFM, still to this day "the only unmarried free slave whom the board sent to the foreign mission field."[15] Though her original desire was to minister in Africa, the calling and assignment of God positioned her to meet the missionary need elsewhere, and with this, she was content. On November 19/20, 1822, Betsey and her new family, the Stewarts, set sail for a five-month voyage to the Sandwich Island (today called Hawaii). Fortunately, Betsey kept a journal. In it she is amazingly honest about the ups and downs of the trip. A few entries from her journal are both enlightening and instructive.[16] Regardless of her conditions, her trust and contentment in Christ are unwavering.

> Nov 20th, 1822—Here begins the history of things known only to those who have bid the American Shores a long adieu.
>
> 21. The weather became stormy, and the sea-sickness commenced.
>
> 23. Saturday morning at daybreak shipped at sea. The water rushed into the cabin. I saw it with very little fear; and felt inclined to say, The Lord reigneth, let us all rejoice. I was so weak that I was almost unable to help myself. At ten o'clock I went on deck: the scene that presented itself was, to me, the most sublime I ever witnessed. How, thought I, can "those that go to the sea in ships" deny the existence of God. The day was spent in self-examination. This, if ever, is the time to try my motives in leaving my native land. I found myself at times unwilling to perish so near my friends; but soon became composed, and resigned to whatever should be the will of my Heavenly Father. I believed that my motives

were pure; and a calm and heavenly peace soon took possession of my breast. Oh that it were always with me as it is this day!

December 1, Sabbath. My soul longed again for the house of the Lord; I endeavored to find him present with me; and soon indeed found that he was near to all that call on him.

30. Sabbath. I felt something of the love of God in my heart. But still I felt as if I was declining in the spiritual life. I attend a little to the study of the Bible, and find it pleasant. Yet I find a void within my breast that is painful.

Jan. 5th, 1823. Sabbath. Pleasant and clear in the morning; a little squally in the afternoon. Had our usual worship. The day was solemn; Mr. Bishop preached for us: but "in vain I sought Him whom my soul loveth." I felt very much inclined to despair, and feared that I had indulged the hope of the hypocrite. Shall I after all become a castaway! Forbid it, O Lord! nor suffer me to injure the cause I have espoused.

Feb. 6th: The weather is beginning to be rather cold. [They traveled all the way down and around South America to go to the Sandwich Islands. The Panama Canal would not be built until 1904–14]. I find my woolen clothes to be very comfortable: my health is very good again—a little homesick, but do not wish to return. O! thought I, if I could but spend one Sabbath evening in your study [of Ashbel Green], how my healer would rejoice. But I must look forward to that as through a glass; and to meet you, with many others in my native land, pray for me. Were it not for that, I should almost despair. I find my heart more deeply corrupted than I had any idea of. I always knew that the human heart was [a] sink of sin, and that mine was filled with it; but I did not know, until now, that the sink was without bottom. I attribute much of my spiritual difficulty to the want of retirement and prayer. It is with the greatest anxiety that I mark the hours as they pass away, which once were devoted to God in secret, without having at present a place for retirement, or indeed at times a heart to retire. Ah! How soon may the people of God grieve away his Holy Spirit. But why should I thus complain and despond. He is still my Father and my God—and I still love him—Yes, my balm is still in Gilead, and my physician there.

Feb. 8.—Here you will indulge me with a passing reflection. I have always remarked, that in the most dangerous situations, I have felt the easiest; and it was because I did not know my danger. And can there be any thing more like a sleeping Christian, or an unawakened sinner? Both in imminent danger, and both stupid. O that God may save me from the spiritual, as he has in mercy from the natural evil.

Feb 9th—I have enjoyed more of the light of my heavenly Father's continence, during the time we were off the Cape, than I ever did in the Atlantic. The only reason I can assign is, that here we have been called hourly to acknowledge his mercy in sparing our lives, and that while we here view his power upon this stormy ocean, we have felt helplessness and been made to adore and tremble. I am not writing to one who is unacquainted with the human heart; you know its dark deceitful nature; and that it is not always kept warm by tender treatment. For me at least it is necessary in order to keep me in my place, to have some doubts, some temptations, and some sickness to struggle with; and even then my garments are far from being kept white. But hitherto has the Lord helped me, and I can raise upon this much dreaded landmark, a strong and lasting Ebenezer. Long, I hope, shall I remember the mercy of my God here. Here too the Spirit of the Lord has, I trust, been striving with some of the sailors, though many are yet, I fear, in the gall of bitterness; some, however, are rejoicing in the Lord. How would your heart rejoice with us, could you see these hearty sons of the ocean, who would scorn to complain of any earthly hardships, bowing with the spirit of children, at the cross of Christ.

16th of February. On the Sabbath, Mr. Richards preached in the cabin, from these words: "Though you made many prayers I will not hear"—warning those that refused to hear the calls of God, of that day when God would refuse to hear them. Oh! How appalling is the thought, that the day is coming, in which we must rise as witnesses against them or they against us—if we have been unfaithful to them. We still retire for fifteen minutes, every evening, directly after publick [sic] prayers, to pray for them—I say retire, that is, we go to different parts of the ship; some of us into the rigging, some out in the boats, and others on the spars; yet in all these places we can find our God.

March 24th—The morning was pleasant, but I could not enjoy it—I was wretched—I could not enjoy my friends, because I could not enjoy my God.

29th—The appearance of the crew has not been so favourable to-day as it was last Saturday. The strong man armed is keeping his palace; but blessed be God there is a stronger than he. Oh! that it would please him to come down and show his power amongst us.

30th—Sabbath. Alas! How unlike those Sabbath mornings I have spent beneath your roof [Ashbel Green], where all was quietness and peace. . . . But I am indulging myself too much in such recollections. I would not, I could not, I dare not, look with longing eyes towards my native land. No sir, my hand lies on the plough, and if my poor wretched heart does not deceive me, I would not take it off for all the wealth of America. It is not the "leeks and the onions" of your land that I long after, but . . . It is spiritual food I want.

On the 24th [of April 1823]. We saw and made Hawaii (Owhyhee). . . . it was not long before objects that were calculated to have a chilling effect of another kind, were brought to our sight. Two or three canoes, loaded with natives, came to the ship: their appearance was that of half man and half beast—naked—except a narrow strip of *tapa* [cloth made from the bark of the paper mulberry tree] round their loins. When they first came on board, the sight chilled our very hearts. The ladies retired to the cabin, and burst into tears; and some of the gentlemen turned pale: my own soul sickened within

> me, and every nerve trembled. Are these, thought I, the beings with whom I must spend the remainder of my life! *They are men and have souls—was the reply which conscience made* [emphasis mine]. I brought my little boy [the Stewart son] on deck, who was two weeks old; some of them took him in their arms, and in ecstasy exclaimed, *araha matitai—very great love to you;* and kissed him. The last expression of affection we could have dispensed with very well; but we have to become all things to all men, that we may gain some.
>
> Near the last of June I had another attack of the pain in my breast, with a little spitting of blood. At the time I was seized, we were without a lancet, or any means of obtaining one, except from a ship that had just come into the harbour. . . . [Found] one from a ship and Mr. R bled me. In a few minutes I was relieved.

Betsey and the Stewarts would begin work immediately. She and the Stewarts went to open a new station at Maui where Betsey would establish a school for ten youths, the first of its kind. In 1824 the mission on Maui opened a school to educate the local chief's servants and family. Betsey Stockton was the first teacher. Her life was hard and lonely. However, Betsey would write, "Though sorrowful, yet I rejoice. The missionary's sorrows and the missionary's joys are mine.—The missionary's grave, and perhaps the missionary's heaven, will also be mine."[17] The ABCFM would give virtually no attention to Betsey Stockton's presence on the mission field. Heaven, however, followed with great interest her every move. And the school Betsey Stockton birthed in Maui took off. "Black History Now" notes that by 1826, eight thousand

Hawaiians had received an education because of the missionary ministry of Betsey.[18] How remarkable for a single black woman, a former slave, who never spent a single day of her life in formal school education. Like Betsey, God will use everyone willing to serve him. Where we are born and the challenges we face are important. But more important is our relationship to God and readiness to be used however he assigns. He can do amazing things with simple servants who are content to please him.

Conclusion

Betsey Stockton would return to America in 1826 with the Stewarts. They were her family, and the poor health of wife and mother Harriett Stewart necessitated this return. However, Betsey Stockton's missionary passion did not wane. It simply went in a new direction.

From 1828–1830, Betsey was hired by the Committee to establish a school for black children in Philadelphia. She would serve as the principal and head teacher. It was the first of its kind.

On July 30, 1829, Betsey would again leave America for mission work in Grape Island, Ontario, Canada. She would teach and help set up the structure of a mission school at Ojibwa. She would instruct the native Indian children. Gregory Nobles writes of her work, "Within two months, the fruits of Stockton's work were apparent—'She came for the purpose of setting up an Infant School, which has succeeded admirably'—and other teachers across the region would build on her success well into the 1830s."[19]

On September 6, 1830, Harriet Stewart died. Betsey took over the personal and direct care of the Stewart's three children and moved them to Princeton. Charles Stewart "graduated with highest honors at the head of his class in the military academy at

West Point and went on to a distinguished career as a brigadier general." He was like a son to Betsey, and she was like a mother to him.[20]

From 1835 to 1865 Betsey lived in Princeton for the remainder of her life. She opened and served as principal at a public (or "common") school for black children. She served "with great distinction for many years."[21] She led the formation of the First Presbyterian Church of Colour of Princeton (later renamed Witherspoon St. Church). She helped found a Sabbath school connected to the church for children and young people and would faithfully teach for twenty-five to thirty years.

Betsey's service to others in Princeton also created amazing fruit in the lives of those around her. Through her recommendation, a seminary student at Princeton, Lewis Mudge, opened a school for working Black men and women to attend at night. Eileen Moffett summarizes well her impact on her community, "'Aunt Betsey' [as her friends called her] grew to be one of Princeton's most admired and beloved figures, though unassuming and gentle in spirit. She had a quiet, steady Christian influence."[22]

On October 24, 1865, Betsey Stockton died a few months after the end of the Civil War and the assassination of Abraham Lincoln. The president of Princeton, John Maclean, conducted her funeral. The great Princeton theologian Charles Hodge also spoke. Her obituary read that her death was "a public loss to the community in which she lived."[23] As we have noted, Betsey was dearly loved by the Stewart family, especially Charles and the children she helped raise. They truly were family, evidenced by the fact that Betsey was buried alongside the Stewart family in Lakewood cemetery in Cooperstown, New York. Her headstone, as Nobles says, "told the outlines of her story."

The grave of
BETSEY STOCKTON,
a native of Princeton N. J.
WHERE SHE DIED
Oct. 24, 1865.
AGED 67 YEARS

Of African blood and born in
Slavery, she became fitted by
education and divine grace,
for a life of great usefulness,
for many years was a
valued missionary at the
Sandwich Islands in the
Family of Rev. C.S. Stewart,
and afterwards till her
death, a popular and able
Principal of Public schools
in Philadelphia & Princeton
honored and beloved by a
large circle of Christian
Friends.[24]

Like Paul, Betsey was fully content in what her heavenly Father had prepared for her. Through every circumstance, in every place, and at any time, she was ready to serve her King. And like Paul, God used this amazing servant of God in wonderful ways. No one could have imagined how God would make her life a life of "firsts" in so many ways. The first unmarried woman to go to the nations. The first single, Black person to go to the nations. The first missionary to start a school for the "common people" of the Sandwich Islands. The first person to start and run a school for infant Black children in Philadelphia. The first teacher in the only school for Black children in Princeton. Biographer Gregory Nobles is right in commenting on her gravestone, "'A life of great usefulness'—a remarkable understatement."[25] But it was the life God planned for his servant Betsey Stockton.

Not I, but Christ in Me—The Victorious Christian Life Exemplified in the Soul-Winning Missionary

Bertha Smith

GALATIANS 2:20

Olive Bertha Smith could be called the unknown or forgotten successor of missionary Lottie Moon. Lottie died on December 24, 1912. Just four and a half years later, the Foreign Mission Board (now the IMB) appointed Bertha Smith. Lottie Moon served in China as a single woman for almost forty years (1873–1912). Bertha Smith would serve in China and Taiwan as a single woman for forty-two years (1917–1958), leaving the mission field at seventy because of a mandatory retirement.

Bertha Smith was a simple, straightforward woman who was born and raised near Cowpens, South Carolina. She was born in the same year Lottie Moon made her initial request for funds that eventually would lead to what we call "The Lottie Moon Christmas Offering for International Missions."

Lewis Drummond refers to Bertha Smith as a "Woman of Revival," and that she was. A spiritual awakening fell on the Shandong Province of China in the late 1920s and "Bertha Smith had no small part in it all."[1] As I studied her life, I could not help but agree with Drummond's perspective. I also could not help being personally convicted by this woman's sacrifice, prayer life, and personal witness. She was a soul-winning machine. May God raise up ten thousand more like her in our day and around the world.

If Bertha Smith had a life verse, it could have been Galatians 2:20: "I have been crucified with Christ, and I no longer live, but Christ lives in me. The life I now live in the body, I live by faith in the Son of God, who loved me and gave himself for me." Or it could have even been Colossians 1:27 which speaks of "Christ in you, the hope of glory." Or perhaps Philippians 1:21, which says, "For me, to live is Christ and to die is gain." Smith packages all three of these verses together in her book *How the Spirit Filled My Life*. She writes,

> God's provision for holy living is Christ enthroned. Positively! The holy life is not our living, it is Christ so freely dwelling at ease in us that He actually can live His life through our personality. We rejoice over Colossians 1:27: "Christ in you, the hope of glory." Christ is in every believer, but that does not mean that all believers are living holy lives. Many are completely defeated. Why? Because the Christ in us does not force Himself over our wills to do anything for us. He waits for us to will that He shall control us. Holy living presupposes death to self—our constantly choosing that position. . . . Living in that position is necessary for holy living. We are never holy if we rebel against Holy God. When we permit the old self to rise up and express itself, or even want

> to, we grieve the One who wants to live His holiness out in us and through us.
>
> Colossians 3:4: "When Christ, who is our life, shall appear. . . ." Philippians 1:21: "For to me to live is Christ." It is Christ enthroned in the heart and life.
>
> Since He lived thus in Paul, He also can live enthroned in you and me, and enable us to say, "I am crucified with Christ: nevertheless I live; yet not I, but Christ liveth in me" (Gal. 2:20).
>
> What kind of life does Christ live in us? A life that is always victorious! That is always at peace and rest! That is equal to any situation which man or the devil and his demons may create!
>
> This is what He wants to do for us.
>
> When experiencing the wars of North China, I learned to pray in every situation, "Now, Lord, you are equal to this!" And He always was! . . . You may say this is not natural. Whoever thought that the Christian life is natural? The Christian life is supernatural. It is God's life in us.[2]

While examining the life of Bertha Smith, I want to zero in on Galatians 2:20. Four marvelous truths are there for our blessing and edification. And each one was beautifully lived out in the life of this incredible missionary.

We Must Live the Crucified Life

Bertha Smith believed "the love of Calvary could not be appreciated until the people had heard the thunder of Sinai."[3]

This captures well the theme of Galatians and the context of our verse.

Paul wants the Galatians to know that law-righteousness (or works-righteousness), justifies no one. As verse 16 makes clear, "We know that a person is not justified by works of the law but by faith in Jesus Christ . . . because by the works of the law no human being will be justified." Therefore as verse 19 declares, "I died to the law, so that I might live for God." Here then is the context of verse 20, a verse Leon Morris said was "personally the most moving text in the whole of Scripture."[4] "I have been crucified with Christ." United with God by faith, Christians share in his death. He died to sin, and we died to sin with him. He died to self on our behalf, and we now die to self for his behalf. There is both an objective and a subjective aspect to this death. The objective looks to our justification. The subjective looks to our sanctification. Objectively, as Tim Keller says, "God treats me just as if I died on the cross and paid for every last sin. I am not liable. So the law has no claim on me. I owe the law nothing. I have paid in full."[5] Subjectively, there is a dying at conversion, and there is a "dying daily" as we grasp the magnitude of our union and identification with my Savior. John Piper puts it so well:

> What does it mean to be crucified with Christ? I think it means this: First, that the gruesome death of the all-glorious, innocent, loving Son of God for my sin is the most radical indictment of my hopeless condition imaginable. The crucifixion of Jesus is the open display of my hellish nature. And, second, when I see this and believe that he really died for me, then my old proud self which loves to display its power by climbing ladders of morality and intellect and beauty and daring dies. Self-reliance and

> self-confidence cannot live at the foot of the cross. Therefore, when Christ died, I died.[6]

Bertha Smith died with Jesus at the age of sixteen, though her struggle began when she was ten. It was on September 5, 1905. In her own words, she writes, "For the first time, I saw that we come to the cross of Christ to be saved. . . . I learned that what the preachers meant by trusting God to save meant to trust God the Son, who settled my sin and my sinful self when He took my sins and me in His own body on the tree."[7]

Responding to a public invitation to come forward, she recounts, "I was on the front seat, having gone forward at the first verse. I knew that I would go; there was no use to wait. It was but a step to where the pastor stood. I took it, gave him my hand to signify that I trusted in Christ's death to save me. By the time I took the second step, which was back to my seat, my years of burden of sin had rolled away, and the joy of the Lord filled my soul."[8]

Bertha Smith lived the crucified life as a Christian. Many examples could be given, but I will note one: her decision to live a single life and serve alone on many occasions on the mission field in China. In her autobiography, following a brief section entitled "Loneliness" (Matt. 28:20), she follows with a section entitled "My Covenant." Here she writes,

> I had been convinced that it was not the Lord's will for me to marry. Up until my second year in China, I had thought that I would be content to live single. How little did I realize what I was saying when I sang so sincerely, "I Surrender All." The Lord gave me a mother heart, the depth of which I had not fathomed, until I saw the difference in the life of a single woman and those who were living with the

one whom they had chosen for a partner, and their own precious children. The married missionaries were in the will of the Lord; why could not such a life be the Lord's will for me? But these questions were answered for me in a very real and transforming experience with the Lord.

I had been in China less than two years when my father passed away in the influenza epidemic of 1918. It was necessary for me to go to Chefoo [pronounced "Chih-fou"], to the nearest U.S. consulate to sign legal papers. This meant eight days of travel there and back. I passed through one mission station going, and another returning, and stayed in the home of missionaries while in Chefoo. By the time I had started on the last stage of the journey back to Laichowfu, I had seen seven happy families with their children. . . .

After leaving the last mission home before reaching my station, I traveled for two days along a lonely road. Realizing what I was going back to, and that this was for life, I wept most of the first day. By the next day I knew that something had to be done. . . .

Calling upon a nearby peak to be my witness, I made a covenant with the Lord: Lord, I want to enter into an agreement with you today. You called me to China and You gave me grace to follow in coming. I am here to win souls for You. The only thing that will take the place of my own children will be spiritual children. If You will take from my heart this pain, I will be willing to go through with just as much inconvenience, self-denial, and pain to see children born into the family of God, as is necessary for a mother to endure for children to be born in the flesh!

In desperation I was calling upon the mighty God for help in facing the difficulties and accepting the compensations of His service, and I was not disappointed.

From that moment forward there were no more tears, for the Lord met my every heart need. I became content with my lot and began to study the Bible and books on soul-winning with a new interest. Prayer became more definite for individuals, and every opportunity to speak for the Lord was seized. The transaction has lasted until this day, and many, many times I have praised the Lord for the privilege of being a single woman with the other person's soul-need having first place in my heart.[9]

We Must Live by Christ Living in Us

Salvation results not only in our identifying with Christ in his death and crucifixion; it also involves our identifying with him in his life and resurrection. As Tom Schreiner writes, "Union with Christ in his death spells the beginning of new life for believers. . . . Believers are now a 'new self' in Christ."[10]

Paul's point here is that the old self, the old man, was crucified. It is no longer "I" who lives. But we are alive. There is a new me. Christ is the animating, energizing person who lives in me. It is indeed "Christ in [me,] the hope of glory" (Col. 1:27). Paul says we are no longer to think of ourselves as living separately from Christ. Christ has become the source, the aim, and the motivating principle of all that we are and all that we do (Phil 1:21).[11]

Bertha Smith believed this truth to be the key to what many call "the victorious Christian life." While some have run amuck into perfectionism with this teaching, Miss Bertha found the balance anchored in Scripture. Commenting on "the all-sufficient Christ who was wanting to live His life in us all the time," she said,

> While we are weak, He wanted to be strength in us.
> While we were stupid, He wanted to be wisdom in us.
> While we were sinful, He wanted to be holiness in us.
> While we were easily aroused and intolerant, He wanted to be patience in us. . . .
> He wanted us to die to self and let Him be our humility.[12]

She found such wisdom essential when enduring persecution and ridicule from the Japanese invaders and the Red (Communist) Army of China. She recalls on one occasion: "The 'Red' influence in the army at that time led the soldiers to ridicule churches and persecute Christians. In a city in Hunan in a street parade, an old beggar man in rags was labeled 'God the Father,' a donkey was labeled 'Jesus,' and an ox, the 'Holy Spirit.'"[13]

Miss Bertha understood that by Christ living in us we would more and more reflect his character, his likeness. In her self-deprecating and folksy manner, she writes, "Children are supposed to favor their parents. Parents are happy for their children to look like them. . . . Through the years when I came home on furloughs, the neighbors who came to greet me invariably said, to my great delight, 'The older Bertha gets, the more she favors her mother.' When I looked around at my beautiful mother to see how she was responding to the thought of her ugly daughter looking like her, I saw the biggest smile on her face."[14] She then adds, "Do people think of Jesus when they see you? Are you holy enough to favor Him?"[15] We must live by Christ living in us. You died with him, and you have been raised with him. Through his Spirit, he is alive in you, and he empowers you to look increasingly more like him!

We Must Live a Life of Faith in Jesus

Jesus does not say, "Change your life, then come to me." He says, "Come to me, and I will change your life." He says to come to him by faith and to live for him by faith. It is the gospel from beginning to end. It is living by faith in the gospel that we are justified, sanctified, and ultimately glorified.

Paul says the new, resurrected person who has Christ living in them continues to live. How? By faith in the One who is the Son of God, deity made flesh, a crucified, risen, and glorified King. This kind of faith in the resurrected Christ sparked what has become known as "The Shandong Revival," which broke out in China 1927. Bertha Smith was in the middle of this mighty movement of God. Former seminary president Lewis Drummond says, "Revival began to permeate the work of the missionaries, although it would be three or four years before the full impact of the awakening would be generally experienced. It spread first among Chinese preachers and Bible-teaching women in the mission schools who were open to seeing themselves in the light of the holiness of God."[16]

Drummond continues,

> Miss Bertha [herself] said that everyone became an evangelist of some sort. All desired to share the

> gospel. Many uneducated farmers became preachers. During the cold winter months when it was impossible for them to work the ground, they would travel by twos to preach Christ throughout the area. So many people professed salvation in Jesus that Dr. Glass (who followed Dr. Culpepper as president of the seminary) and pastor Kwan, (president of the North China Baptist Convention) felt constrained to tour a number of villages to help the numerous converts. Glass and Kwan were often kept up all night just reading the Word of God to the many new believers. Such was the spirit among those born again.[17]

Wes Handy builds on Drummond and summarizes "The Revival among Missionaries."[18] In the safety of the port Chefoo in the year 1927, Southern Baptist missionaries gathered for spiritual renewal while the turmoil in the province continued. As they passed the time, Jane Lide shared lessons she had learned from a Bible study while on furlough in Southern California on "Christ Our Life." The missionaries spent much time in Bible study and prayer. They began to pray for revival among the Chinese, but God convicted them of their own need for revival. Marie Monsen, a Norwegian Evangelical Lutheran missionary with the China Inland Mission, shared with the Baptists of her experiences in the interior.

One of the Southern Baptists, Ola Culpepper, suffered from a degenerative eye disease, which was causing her extreme pain. None of the doctors could treat her disease. She simply changed prescriptions. The missionaries had heard of Monsen's experiences with healing and asked her to pray for Ola. C. L. Culpepper relates that at the meeting with Monsen, she posed him the question, "Brother Culpepper, have you been filled with the Holy Spirit?" (This question sent him on a lengthy quest that would find fruition in the spiritual awakening to come.) The missionaries met, read aloud James 5:14–16, and being impressed by James's exhortation to confess sin, anointed Ola's head with oil and prayed for her healing. Bertha Smith shares that as she went to lay hands on Mrs. Culpepper's head, she could not because she was convicted of a negative attitude toward fellow missionary Anna Hartwell. Concurrently, two Chinese cooks whose hatred toward one another was well known had reconciled in the adjacent room. During the prayer, Ola Culpepper put down her glasses and her eyes never bothered her again. Soon afterwards, the missionaries were given freedom to return to the villages, but Marie Monsen's question to Dr. Culpepper would not go away.

> After much study of Acts, Galatians 3:14, and Ephesians, the missionaries were convinced that they were not ministering in the fullness of the Holy Spirit. According to Mary Crawford,
>
> For several years there had been an increasing hunger in the hearts of most of us to see more of the Power of the Holy Spirit in our work. We had been taught in our seminaries that if we ever got any souls saved it would be through the work of the Holy Spirit. We knew the doctrine of the Acts of the Apostles, but we were not experiencing it as we knew we should. After the Chinese Southern Army came in during the year 1928, and so much of our work showed up as "hay and stubble" most of us were willing to "humble ourselves under the mighty hand of God that He might exalt us in due season."[19]

Bertha Smith tells of her struggle to overcome the sin within her. She had experienced fillings of the Spirit before coming to China, but it would be in those days in Chefoo that she would learn to allow "the Holy Spirit a chance to so control the old self that it [the old self] was ineffective over [her]."[20] One missionary would confess that she had never been a "saved" Christian.

It took C. L. Culpepper four years to cleanse himself through prayer before he would receive the fullness of the Holy Spirit. He had been afraid of the excesses and was afraid to speak in tongues and to be put out of the SBC. But in Hwanghsien, "He gathered with forty Christians to pray for revival and he fell under conviction of the 'sin of not being filled with the Holy Spirit.'" He confessed before the people "the sin of accepting praise as a good missionary while knowing he was far from God. This prayer meeting reportedly lasted for four days and four nights with people coming under conviction and confessing their sins. Toward the end of that meeting, the Chinese brothers said, 'We thought you considered yourselves above us. Now we are all one.'"[21] They knew they were no longer separated as Chinese and Americans but finally united as God's children.

Wiley Glass was at the meeting in Hwanghsien. He saw the face of a man, whom he hated, come before him, who years before had insulted his first wife. God dealt with his heart. "After gradually coming to confess the full sin, he wept and felt the fullness of forgiveness: 'When repentance washed the guilt away and the peace of forgiveness filled my soul, I knew an ecstacy [sic] of joy beyond description.'"[22]

The reports of Southern Baptist missionaries being filled with the Spirit must have been disturbing to the leaders back in the U.S. The journal of the FMB, *Home and Foreign Fields*, from 1932 to 1933 was filled with reports of the revival. One missionary remarked,

> I have come into the midst of revival fires in China—marvelous, wonderful, deep is the work of the Holy Spirit here. Oh, that the fire might fall amongst Southern Baptists of America! I came up to Hwanghsien ["Haungshan"] from Tsining for a few days and I have never seen a place so transformed. The first delightful thing I noticed was the warmth and genuineness of the cordial welcome of the Chinese. They seem to have had a baptism of love that flows out of their very countenances. The spirit of worship and praise and reverence in the church service Sunday surpassed anything I saw or felt in America.[23]

These reports would provoke suspicion from the FMB leaders in Richmond, with the accusation being "the missionaries had indulged in Pentecostal excess."[24] In 1935, the executive secretary of the Foreign Mission Board, Charles E. Maddry, visited North China Mission and came back with glowing reports. His main points defended the validity of the work by the missionaries: "First. A good foundation for Christ's church has been laid. . . . Second. Our missionaries who are building on this foundation today are worthy, devoted and sacrificial. . . . Third. The superstructure they are building is glorious. . . . Fourth. The material for present and future building is superior and unlimited."[25] Handy notes that he directly defended the North China Mission when he said,

> In the great revival that has swept through North and Interior China, there have been some excesses and hysteria, but it is rapidly passing today. Our missionaries have their feet on the solid rock of Christ Jesus and they are building gloriously on the

> foundation laid so deep and strong by those heroes and martyrs who preceded them. . . . A glorious revival is sweeping Northern and Interior China, such as we have not seen in America in a hundred years. We have seen it and felt its power. It is a revival of fire and burning. Sin is being burned out of broken lives and men and women are being absolutely made over. The power of Christ has come to grips with the power of Satan and it is a fearful conflict. Satan has held sway and dominion over China for unnumbered and weary centuries. His kingdom is suddenly being challenged and broken by the power of a risen and enthroned Christ.[26]

We must live a life of faith in Jesus. It will challenge us. It will take us out of our comfort zone. And it will be worth it. God will amaze us what he accomplishes in us for his glory. Bertha Smith saw this firsthand in the Shantung Revival. Her life was changed. Her resolve to serve Christ no matter what was settled.

We Must Live in the Reality of the Atoning Love of the Son of God

"The Son of God loved me and gave himself for me." What a wonderful gospel truth that is. Paul, of course, does not deny that Jesus loves us today. He certainly does. Paul is simply looking back to that decisive event at Calvary. John Piper says, "Paul was utterly mastered, held captive, by one great scene in history: a cross on Golgotha, and on it, the Son of God who loved us and gave himself for us."[27]

Bertha Smith was utterly mastered by the cross. She never doubted the specific, personal, and particular love Christ had for her and the millions of Chinese she longed to see saved. That is why she was a 24/7 walking, talking, breathing soul-winner, the likes of whom we have seldom seen. First, she writes that "women on the mission field often have to do the work which men do not go to do."[28] She went and did the work of an evangelist!

Second, she says,

> Day after day I went to the bus terminal, stood at a loading stop, and took out a tract in Chinese and started reading it. The long line of waiting passengers would look amazed, and one would ask, "Do you know what you are reading?" When I answered, "Yes, would you like to know?" he would reach for a tract and then the whole line would follow suit. When that bus loaded, I moved to the next outgoing one. Often I had a chance for enough conversation to secure a card with address, or I repeated, in my mind, the name and address given me, until the person had turned away, and I could record it in my notebook.[29]

Third, Bertha Smith says, "I put my name in both English and Chinese on the bamboo fence: 'Miss Smith Baptist Mission.' People began to come. In addition to the Sunday services, we had Bible classes Tuesday and Thursday evenings. . . . People came for help until I need never have left my home to put in a day's work for the Lord. My sofa was literally ruined by the tears of repentance shed on it, but to me it was only beautifully brocaded."[30]

Fourth, she wanted everybody to be saved. "The Lord laid on my heart twenty unsaved young people about my age. I began to pray for them by name daily and saw eighteen of them saved that same summer. The nineteenth was saved some years later. The other one moved away and I lost contact."[31]

Fifth, "Here come some girls, some new converts, saying that a new girl wants to be saved and asked if they can bring her in here to pray. They said they feared that I would be taking a nap at this time. It is just after dinner. I told them to come in. I would dispense with the nap. They rushed out joyfully to bring her. Lots and lots of love, and a heart full of thanks to you for all that you have done for me, and taught me and meant to me."[32]

When the Great Depression hit and the Foreign Mission Board could not fund her return to China following her furlough, she returned anyway on faith, trusting in Christ to provide. And he did! When forced to leave China when Communism took over, she did not return home, but in 1948 became the first FMB appointed missionary to Formosa (Taiwan).

Following her "forced retirement," she did mission work in Australia, Burma, Ghana, India, Indonesia, Israel, Japan, Korea, Lebanon, Nigeria, the Philippines, South America, and Zimbabwe. However, she had no bitterness about her retirement and with remarkable wisdom wrote, "I felt that I was just then qualified from experience for missionary work. The forty-one and a half years had been very short, interesting indeed, at times thrilling, and always rewarding. Every trial along the way had been forgotten as soon as the next person was saved. However, I agreed with the Foreign Mission Board, that its retirement policy was good. Since the mind that we know with grows old, too, some of us would never be willing to retire, were it left to our discretion."[33]

In her own words hear the heart of this great lady so captivated by the love of the One who lived inside her and gave himself for her: "There are many Mohammedans in this part of China. The Bible woman asked me how such a religion could spread from Arabia here and get such a hold. Is it because the followers of the false prophet are more zealous for him than we are for our Lord, or is it that the sinful human heart can more readily accept the false than the true? Perhaps it is both."[34]

Bertha Smith's faith in God's care and providence is truly amazing. When the war raged around her and bombs blew up portions of her home and bullets whistled thru her bedroom, here was her response:

> One afternoon when returning from my visit to the hospital, I found even the Christians in great excitement over the bomb that had been dropped just across the narrow street from our grounds. I kept quoting to them, "God is our refuge and strength. . . . Therefore we will not fear, though the earth be removed (Ps. 46:1–2). It meant something when I stood with them and quoted it.
>
> My own favorite was John 14:20; "I am in my Father, and you in me, and I in you," said Jesus. How safe! Anything touching me would have to pass by God the Father, then it would have to get by Jesus Christ the Son, before it could reach me; and if it did, there would be the Lord inside of me, so filling me with Himself that there would be no problem. What the Chinese friends called courage, boldness, strength, was Christ Himself living His life in me. Now you may be sure that I had my sins forgiven [and] up to date at such a time! I was not only keeping clean enough inside for Him to dwell, but I was choosing His will in advance, daily and moment by moment.
>
> Since Christ was faithful to the one who was trusting Him, every day was filled with joy, with

> never a thought of what might happen, or of any personal danger. I was in the place to which the Lord had brought me, and if I should die with the others, it did not matter. I was completely possessed with the desire to do all that I could, for all the people that I could, while I could, for the night would surely come.[35]
>
> As we went around busily, the Chinese co-workers would ask, "Why did God, in whom we were trusting, permit those bombs to drop here on our mission grounds?"
>
> I had known the Lord since before they were born and could answer, "We never ask 'Why' about anything that God permits. He knew that we were here and He knew that we were trusting Him. We may not understand in this life, but this is not evil. The Lord permitted this for some purpose. He, the mighty God, does not have to explain Himself to human beings—at least not now.[36]

And once more, "I had been in China for twenty-five years and during that time had learned, when anything new and unexpected came up, to get on my knees and turn it over to the Lord just as soon as possible. The problem then became His responsibility, and I was saved from the worry of it."[37] Bertha never moved her eyes off Jesus's finished work on the cross. Because he died, she had to tell others about him. Because he was raised from the dead, she would spend her whole life spreading his name among the nations.

Conclusion

Just a few weeks shy of her hundredth birthday, Bertha Smith died on June 12, 1988. Right up to the time of her death, she continued to care and pray for "her children" in China.[38] When she retired from active missionary service, the number of believers in China was estimated at approximately five million. At her death, the number had swelled to between fifty and seventy million! The Shandong Revival has been credited for sparking much of the increase.[39] After being required to retire, she continued to serve our Lord for another twenty-nine years. Her cousin Pamela Reid said she was "truly an angel of light." On her tombstone you will find the inscription of Proverbs 3:6, "In All Thy Ways Acknowledge Him, and He Shall Direct Thy Paths."

As she was about to leave America to head for China in 1917, at the age of twenty-nine, Bertha Smith wrote in a letter these words, "My heart rejoices that I am on the way to China. I feel unworthy of the privilege of going . . . but I am trusting that God shall use me to do a great work for Him there."[40] Missionary Jim Elliot said something similar when he wrote in a letter to his parents, "Missionaries are very human folks, just doing what they are asked. Simply a bunch of nobodies trying to exalt somebody."[41]

When it comes to her trust in a great God to somehow do a great work through her life, Bertha Smith was not disappointed! May our sovereign God raise up an army of men and women who will follow in Miss Bertha's footsteps, die to self, allow Christ to live in and through them, live a life of radical faith, and be moved to serve by the truth that we are forever loved by Jesus. How do we know? The cross! It tells us so.

8

A Slave of All—the Heart of

Charlotte Atlee White Rowe,

America's First Appointed Female Missionary to the Nations

1 CORINTHIANS 9:19, 22–23

Charlotte Hazen Atlee (1782–1863) would lose both her parents by age eleven and become an orphan. As we will discover in the coming pages, she would marry Nathaniel White (1803) only to lose her husband shortly past their first wedding anniversary and her nine-month-old son a short while later. In God's providence she would sail to Southeast Asia on December 20, 1815, as America's first appointed female missionary. Death would continue to be her constant companion for the rest of her life, but so would the heart of a missionary. In her application letter for missionary appointment written in 1815, she writes, "Since the date of my conversion, I humbly hope my desire has been to do good, and glorify my Redeemer, and especially since missionary endeavors have come within my knowledge, I have felt myself deeply interested in them; and their success has been the constant subject of my prayers."[1]

Charlotte would never lose her heart for the nations even though her path to the mission field and life on the field was not easy. She would face opposition on the field and lack of support back home because she was a single woman, a widowed missionary. Still, like the apostle Paul, she was committed to make herself "a slave to everyone" (1 Cor 9:19) that she "may by every possible means save some" (1 Cor 9:22). These verses capture the heart of Charlotte Atlee White Rowe. Three truths in particular stand out from this text and her life.

Become a Slave to All to Win Them to Christ

(1 CORINTHIANS 9:19)

First Corinthians 9 is about an unpopular subject in our day: surrendering your rights to serve others. Paul has in mind a particular act of surrender for the follower of Jesus. It is a surrender of our rights for the sake of the gospel and the souls of the lost. Paul writes in verse 19, "Although I am free from all and not anyone's slave, I have made myself a slave to everyone, in order to win more people." Laying down our rights for the salvation of others is an easy decision to make for the Savior who purchased us by his blood (1 Cor. 6:20; 7:23). We do for others what Jesus has done for us. Warren Wiersbe puts it well: "What a paradox: free from all men [because I belong to Christ], and yet the servant of all men [because I belong to Christ]!"[2]

The heart of a servant is on beautiful and visible display in Charlotte Atlee White Rowe throughout the eighty-two years our Lord gave her.[3] She was born the last of eleven children on July

13, 1782. Tragically, her mother died at forty-two, just before Charlotte's eighth birthday. Three years later her father died of yellow fever. Charlotte was now an orphan, and she likely went to live with her oldest sister Elizabeth.[4] Charlotte would marry Nathaniel White on Thursday, November 17, 1803. He was twenty-nine, and she was twenty-one. They were blessed with a son the next year, but a double tragedy soon struck. Nathaniel died on December 25, 1804, at the age of thirty, and their baby boy passed away five months later at nine months of age.[5] Charlotte would move to Haverhill, Massachusetts, the home of her husband, and here she would come to know her Savior.

Charlotte was converted under the evangelical preaching of the Baptist pastor William Batchelder. In her application letter to the Baptist Board of Foreign Missions, she writes, "I was led to search the Scriptures in order to find assurance that Jesus Christ is the Son of God; in doing which, I was blessed with a desire to be converted from darkness to light; the Holy Spirit rousing me to repent and enabling me to confess Christ as my Lord and Savior."[6] Charlotte would be baptized at age twenty-three on June 29, 1806. As she stepped into the waters, she spontaneously began to sing, much to the disapproval of some "proper Congregationalist[s]."[7]

From the moment of her conversion, a missionary passion began to beat in Charlotte's heart. It is almost certain she was influenced by the missionaries Harriett Newell and Ann Judson since their lives overlapped and they lived in the same geographical region. Further, her church in Philadelphia (Samson Street Baptist) and its pastor William Staughton were strongly mission-minded. In May 1814, Baptists from eleven states and Washington D.C. came together in Philadelphia to form the General Missionary Convention of the Baptist Denomination in the United States of America for Foreign Missions, which was also known as the Triennial Convention. Charlotte White would help form and lead the Samson Street Baptist Female Society for Promoting Evangelical Missions. This is one of the earliest women's missionary societies in America.[8] As a leader, Charlotte held the title vice-directress. However, in her heart, she yearned to go.

In 1815, Charlotte White applied to become a missionary to Burma and accompany George and Phebe Hough. Her application came with significant controversy. She was a single woman, and only ordained men could be appointed missionaries at the time. Even wives of male missionaries did not receive the appointment of missionary. Charlotte was neither a feminist nor a troublemaker. She simply wanted to go for her King and save souls. When the mission board informed her they had no funds to support her, Charlotte said she would support herself. She would donate her modest estate to the mission board as a financial contribution to fund her own missionary service.[9] Her humility and wisdom are also evident in her response to the mission board: "My wishes are to reside in [the Hough's] family in the character of a sister to Mrs. Hough and a sister in the Lord."[10] Trulson is most certainly correct in setting the context for this significant moment:

> Charlotte understood that God was calling her to something other than childcare. She desired to travel to Burma with the Hough's [sic] "to pursue such studies as are requisite to the discharge of missionary duties." Lest the men of the board misunderstand, Charlotte wrote that she expected "to apply what talents I possess wholly to the service of the mission, either in the management of a school, or to hold private meetings, should there be opportunity, with the native females, to instruct them in the principles of the gospel, hoping, by the blessing of God, that

> some of them will be raised from their degraded and miserable condition to participate in the riches of salvation."
>
> Charlotte explained that she had previously "been excluded from rendering any service to the mission, but I now rejoice that God has opened a way." She had no family obligations. She had the Staughtons' support. She was an experienced educator. And she could sail safely to Asia in the company of the Hough family.
>
> The Board considered her application, and on June 14, 1815, voted its approval. Charlotte Hazen Atlee White had become the first American woman to receive official appointment by any sending body to serve as an international, cross-cultural missionary.[11]

Charlotte gladly became a slave to all, even to her brothers in Christ who stood in her way and opposed her going to the nations, that she "might win more of them" for the Savior she so loved and adored. On December 20, 1815, she and the Houghs left America to head to India. They would arrive in Calcutta on April 23, 1816, after 129 days at sea. Charlotte immediately set herself to the task of winning souls, particularly those of women and children.

Deny Yourself for Others to Win Them to Christ

(1 CORINTHIANS 9:22)

Verses 19 and 22 have a similar perspective and are complementary in nature. Paul will do whatever he must, as a slave to

Christ, to win Jews and Gentiles to the Savior. He will also do whatever he can to win those he calls "the weak" (v. 22). These are new believers who have come out of paganism and idolatry and are still growing in their faith. Paul says, "I have become all things to all people, so that I may by every possible means save some." Such an attitude and disposition are essential for children of God, especially those who understand they are on mission for the Savior. Charlotte White would exemplify this mindset to the fullest. No doubt the counsel of her pastor in Philadelphia, William Staughton, gave her direction: "Be willing to be any thing, provided the cause for which you give up the endearments of your natal soil and home, may be promoted." And, concerning the fact she would not be funded by the mission board, he encouraged her: "Never despair with Jesus for your leader."[12]

Charlotte arrived in Calcutta on April 23, 1816, and remained with the Houghs for only two months. She met and married a missionary widower with three sons named Joshua Rowe (1781–1823). The wedding took place on June 11, 1816. Joshua's wife Elizabeth had died on October 19, 1814, after giving birth to their second daughter, Elizabeth Maria, who also died. Both were buried next to daughter Eliza, previously deceased. Joshua was under appointment with the British Baptist Missionary Society (BMS). Having been appointed (amid ongoing controversy) back home, Charlotte now asked to be appointed as a missionary with the BMS. They turned her down, though recognizing her as the wife of a missionary. Back home in America, the mission board's next actions were shameful. Without Charlotte's knowledge, the board "resigned" her in December 1816. She knew nothing of this action. In fact, she had hoped to maintain "some filial affinity" with her spiritual family back home.[13] It would be two more years, April 16, 1819, before the American Mission Board would return Charlotte's previous donation to cover her missionary service.[14]

Joshua, Charlotte, and the three boys made their way to Digha, India, where the Rowes had served since 1811. Charlotte immediately began learning the language for preparation in the area of education. Writing home to Philadelphia, she challenged other women to follow after her, exhorting them, "The support of schools is the bread of the mission, and the *power of truth.* In this respect, the labour of females is highly important."[15] Concerning her own feelings in this matter, Charlotte wrote to her pastor back home, telling him her heart was "to devote my every talent to the gracious Giver, and to serve his cause all my days and hours."[16]

Charlotte White Rowe excelled as an educator in India. She quickly learned the language, and by December 1816 she was speaking and writing Hindi. She also was soon managing three schools. Eventually she and her husband would oversee ten such works. Trulson provides an excellent summation of their missionary philosophy: "Charlotte and Joshua believed that schools were an important form of mission and saw them as 'an excellent method of spreading divine truth.' They recognized the distinction between intellectual knowledge *about* Jesus and a personal relationship *with* Jesus. Education about the Christian faith could prepare students to enter that living relationship. It could also be a means of introducing the good news of Jesus in students' villages and families."[17]

"Evangelism by education" is an apt description of their method. They worked together as a marvelous team, and Charlotte thrived in her "missionary work among the women and children," as Joshua called it. In a letter to a man named John Saffey, Joshua Rowe wrote of his wife: "I wish she were freed from her school altogether, and had the whole of her time to devote to Missionary work among the native females. She is becoming more qualified for such an employment every day, and I hope something will turn up to free her from her present engagements in the school, and to enable her to devote herself *entirely* to *Missionary* work. This is the specific object for which she came to India and this is the work in which she wishes both to live and to die."[18]

In one significant area Charlotte Rowe's missiology stands out: her attention of the Indians in their specific geographical and cultural location. She was convinced, given dialectical differences and variations, that language was best learned on the field among and from native speakers ("becoming all things to all peoples"). Her counsel was "that missionaries should learn from Indigenous language guides speaking their mother tongue."[19] Adapting culturally and linguistically is the job of the missionaries, not those they have come to serve and save. In this regard, "Charlotte was addressing a missiological issue that would far out-live her time."[20]

Let the Gospel Be Your Motivation to Win Others to Christ

(1 CORINTHIANS 9:23)

Gospel is a crucial term in the book of 1 Corinthians, especially this chapter. The word *euangelion* occurs eleven times in the book, with nine occurrences appearing in chapter 9. Paul clearly and precisely defines the gospel for us in 1 Corinthians 15:3–6. "The gospel is the good news that King Jesus died and paid the full penalty of sin, rose bodily from the dead, and saves all who repent of their sin and trust only in him."[21] The gospel above all was the motivating impulse for the apostle Paul. As he so succinctly puts it, "I do all this [see vv. 19–22] because of [ESV, "for the sake of"] the gospel." And his motive is an evangelistic one: "so that I may share in the blessings," the blessings of saving some (v. 22). Charlotte Rowe's heart pulsed with the same passion as the apostle, the same passion as her beloved Savior (Mark 10:45;

Luke 19:10). It was a passion that would lead her to travel roads of blessing, sorrow, disappointment, perseverance, and sacrifice.

Charlotte and Joshua Rowe together would have three children to add to the three Joshua brought from his first marriage. Twin daughters would be born on October 20, 1818. Their names were Charlotte Elizabeth and Esther Anna. In April 1823 they would add a son they named Edwin Atlee. They were now a family of eight. Sadly, sorrow was just around the corner. In September 1823, Joshua became severely ill. On September 21 he preached a farewell sermon to his church at Dinapore. Three weeks later he called his children and wife to his bedside, kissed them, and assured them they would all be united in heaven with their Lord and Savior. In the meantime, God would be their Father. Joshua died on October 11, 1823. He was forty-one years old.

Charlotte herself was ill and not sure she would live. Add to that the burden of caring for six children ages seventeen to seven months, it is a wonder she survived. But she would both survive and thrive against odds that would have beaten most of us. She went to Calcutta to recuperate and find jobs for the older boys. She returned to Digha to find the mission station in disrepair. But "[l]ike the wise business-woman of Proverbs 31, Charlotte used industry and investment to tackle the problems."[22] She rebuilt and renovated the mission station. For the next three years she supervised the schools and church, doing so out of her own resources. She received neither a salary nor funding from America or England. Undeterred, she did the missionary work of evangelist, educator, and pastor, though she had no illusions or desire to take the office of a pastor or elder. For want of a man, she took all the burdens of a missionary on her shoulders in humble service to her King "for the sake of the gospel." For eleven years, Charlotte Rowe raised money and used her personal funds to sustain the work to which God had called her. As she wrote to John Dyer in 1824, "My own head and hand have everything to decide and perform."[23]

Charlotte diligently supported two Indian evangelists named Hurree Das and Roop Das. So blessed were the two men by Charlotte's care and counsel they referred to her as "their pastoress."[24] In this regard she was much like Sarah Boardman Judson and Lottie Moon who were forced to step in when no man was to be found to do the pastoral work.

Though she worked tirelessly to give her attention to all manner of ministry needs, Charlotte eventually found herself alone, all her funds now depleted. Her three young children had each been seriously ill on multiple occasions. The fear of her own death caused her great anxiety for her little ones. What would happen to them if she were to die? Trulson explains their situation well:

> Joshua [her husband] had received no salary that could be continued to her. And because the society had not recognized her as an appointed missionary, she had no salary of her own. For ten years, first under American Baptists and then under British Baptists, she had self-funded her missionary service. Her dependents included her three stepsons, her twin daughters, her son, and Ramkisoon's widow. The society had given some modest grants to support the nine mission schools under her oversight, but as the grants were not sufficient, she supported the Digha girls' school herself. Charlotte also paid the wages of Sarah Bacon, who taught Charlotte's children and two young girls Charlotte had taken in to educate.
>
> Charlotte was ready to live and die a missionary in India. She told John Dyer, "I am content to be here

> for life. Nay I expect to bury my bones here." She was torn, knowing that her resolve to follow God's call to be a missionary also affected her children. She confided this inner struggle to her mother-in-law: "I remain in the mission because I am a missionary, and would prefer dying such—but out of the mission I could lay up a little future support for my babes. My duty to them, might urge the latter, to a worldly mind—but I have a trust in God, that though we remain poor, he will keep my children alive and from the examples of the wicked, this is my chief concern.[25]

The lack of support from back home and deteriorating health necessitated a difficult decision for Charlotte. She would go to England to regain her health and also meet with the British Mission Society and appeal in person for sufficient support to return to India and continue the work. She delayed her journey until she had raised sufficient funds to pay her own way and that for her three youngest children. She would not be a financial burden to the BMS. She left November 1, 1826, with every desire and intention to return. In God's providence that would not happen. Even with the support of William Carey, the BMS determined she would be responsible to raise her own support if she was to return to the work in India.[26]

Without missionary appointment or support, Charlotte, a poor widow with children, returned to America on September 23, 1829. There is no record of a word of bitterness or criticism about either Baptist mission board in Britain or America. Charlotte would go on to open a boarding school for girls in Philadelphia, living a simple and meager life. In 1830 she began writing articles for *The Columbian Star* and *Christian Index* under the titles "Hints to Young Friends of Missions" and "Scenes in India—Addressed to the Young."[27] In these articles she challenged her young readers to support missions and consider missionary service themselves.

Charlotte Rowe would live briefly in Lowndesboro, Alabama, before returning to Pennsylvania where she would serve as the principal of Strasburg Female Seminary in Strasburg, Pennsylvania, just south of Lancaster. The year was 1850. Charlotte would have been sixty-two years old. Tragically, her daughter Esther would die in March 1851 at age thirty-two. A year and a half later, in October 1852, her daughter Charlotte would die at age thirty-four. The twin daughters are buried next to each other in the cemetery of St. James Episcopal Church in Lancaster. At this point, Charlotte Atlee White Rowe quietly disappears from the historical record. In many ways, the often-quoted phrase "Preach the gospel, die, and be forgotten" explains the life of an orphan girl from Lancaster, Pennsylvania, and missionary to India named Charlotte Atlee White Rowe.[28]

Conclusion

Charlotte Atlee White Rowe's last years are shrouded in mystery. However, her legacy tells a different and rather amazing story. Trulson provides the details of Charlotte Atlee White Rowe's life of faithful service as a missionary to India and its continuing impact:

> Her stepsons Joshua and Josiah Rowe both found ways to serve in India. Joshua had hoped to assist her in re-establishing the female schools at Digah upon her return to India. Although that hope never materialized, Joshua worked at the mission press in Serampore and then became an English tutor at

Fort William College. . . . [He worked] alongside William Carey and Joshua Marshman, who were on the faculty. . . . His brother Josiah was a trustee of the Lall Bazar Baptist Chapel in Calcutta and a member of the governing committee of the Calcutta Baptist Missionary Society, an auxiliary to the Baptist Missionary Society of London. Josiah . . . was the architect for the chapels at the Boys' Native Christian Institution in Entally and at the Jan Bazar in Calcutta. He contributed generously to the costs of both chapels and for expansion of the Circular Road Baptist Church in Calcutta. Charlotte's step-grandson Joshua Mardon Rowe studied Persian, Arabic, Bengali, Urdu, and Hindi to prepare for missionary service but died in Agra in 1852 at age twenty-one before being appointed. Her step-granddaughter Rhoda Mardon Rowe served in Allahabad, India, with her missionary husband, Thomas Evans.

Charlotte's American family was likewise active in mission. Her niece Harriet Hildreth Morse worked for seven years in Siam. After failing health forced Harriett to return to the United States in 1855, she resumed ministry among Native Americans by becoming matron at the Baptist mission school for the Delaware nation in Kansas. . . . Charlotte's grandnephew Daniel Appleton White Smith (D. A. W. Smith) sailed to Burma in 1863. Smith served in Burma for fifty-two years, first at Henzada and then for forty years as president of the Karen Theological Seminary at the Rangoon suburb of Insein. A thousand men trained for the ministry under his guidance.[29]

This would be a remarkable legacy as it is, but there is still more that came as a result of Charlotte's life and ministry as a missionary. Trulson notes, "Because Charlotte had dared to open the door for women to be appointed as missionaries, her influence extended beyond the ministries of her own family. More than half of the 386 missionaries sent out by the Baptist Board in its first fifty years were wives or single women."[30]

On Christmas Day 1863 Charlotte Hazen Atlee White Rowe died at the age of eighty-two, "the same day on which her first husband had died fifty-nine years earlier. Charlotte's body was carried from Philadelphia to St. James Episcopal Church in Lancaster, Pennsylvania, where her funeral service was held on December 27th. She was buried in plot #9 of St. James cemetery next to her twin daughters."[31] America's (and Baptists') first appointed woman foreign missionary was laid to rest, without earthly notice or attention, in an unmarked grave. I strongly suspect it was otherwise in heaven. Like Stephen in Acts 7, I can easily imagine our Savior standing to welcome his precious daughter home, allowing her to fall into the loving embrace of the Lord she so passionately loved and devotedly spent her life serving, that by all means some may be saved. Charlotte's life was a life worth living. It is also a life worth remembering for the glory of King Jesus.

9

With All Your Heart—A Life of Faithful Trust and Obedience Beautifully Exemplified in Missionary

Yvette Aarons

PROVERBS 3:5–8

Yvette Aarons is a marvelous trophy of God's amazing grace. She is also an example of someone who has returned again and again to the wisdom and promises in Proverbs 3:5–8 for strength and guidance. Born deaf and Black and not knowing her earthly father, she would find the love and acceptance of a heavenly Father through His Son Jesus and become the first deaf missionary ever appointed by the Foreign Mission Board (FMB), now the International Mission Board (IMB) of the Southern Baptist Convention. Her road was not easy, but the hand of divine providence accompanied her every step of the way. As Yvette says, "You don't have to be smart, strong or courageous, but you need to be obedient! That is all, and that is who Jesus and the world needs."[1]

Ray Ortlund says Proverbs 3 "is an education in life at its best. . . . God is speaking to us as his beloved ones, his adopted children. . . . He chose us, because he loves us, and now he is coaching us in how we can be fully alive for his glory."[2] Proverbs 3:5–6 are probably the most well-known verses in this entire book of wisdom, given by a father to his son (1:8). These are life verses for one of King Jesus's most remarkable daughters, Yvette Aarons. Wisdom flows from these verses for all of God's children.

Trust the Lord Fully

(PROVERBS 3:5)

Verses 5–8 build on the commands and promises of verses 1–4. We are admonished not to forget the LORD's teachings but to let our hearts keep his commandments (v. 1). If we do, our days will be extended, and peace will be our companion (v. 2). We should hold closely to the Lord's steadfast love and faithfulness (v. 3). If we do, we "will find favor and high regard with God and people" (v. 4). In verse 5, Solomon commands us to "trust in the LORD [Yahweh]" and to do so to the fullest, "with all your heart." The word "trust" "carries the force of relying on someone for security; [here] the confidence is to be in the Lord and not in human understanding. . . . The call is for a trust characterized by total commitment—with all your heart."[3] The negative parallel to this trust follows quickly in the second half of verse 5, "And do not rely on your own understanding." Divine guidance and wisdom should always trump human counsel and thinking. We must not lean on the "broken crutch" of our own understanding and the "thimble of [our] knowledge."[4] Eugene Peterson puts the whole verse well: "Trust GOD from the bottom of your heart; don't try to figure out everything on your own" (*The Message*). Yvette Aarons's life is a wonderful testimony to a life lived in trusting obedience to this verse.

Yvette was born in Jamaica on May 31, 1959. Both of her parents were able to hear, and neither were Christians. Sadly, she never knew her earthly father. She is the oldest of three girls. She also had a brother, but he died at three months old. Born deaf, Yvette says that she did not understand much as a child. However, in a neighborhood Sunday school class at an early age, she was taught John 3:16 and began to memorize Scripture, a practice she continues to this day.[5] Her missionary friend Vesta Sauter says she was avid at memorizing Scripture.[6] Although John 3:16 was shared with her at an early age, Yvette did not understand everything at that time.[7] But God had a plan for this little girl that virtually no one could have envisioned for her.

A church with a bus ministry, Rehoboth Gospel Assembly, began coming by Yvette's home and would pick her up. When she was twelve, this large church taught her the Bible, emphasized Scripture memorization, and gave Christmas gifts for memorizing God's Word. At fifteen, Yvette began attending worship services, "big church" as she called it. She remembers being moved watching the pastor kneel and pray.[8] God was working in her heart. After church one Sunday, she went forward and told the pastor she wanted Jesus. She did not understand all her pastor said, but she knew she was putting her trust in God.[9] Yvette was sixteen when she was converted, and she began to follow Jesus with her whole heart. She was baptized in a nearby church along with a queue of deaf believers since the deaf missionary church did not own a baptistry.

Yvette continued to grow in the Lord. This time is also when God gave her the dream of someday becoming a missionary. Yvette became interested in missions shortly after her conversion. She attended the only deaf church in the area, which had American missionaries that signed differently when they taught and preached. However, Yvette was grateful. "They had come to live with us and teach us about Jesus!"[10] Watching missionaries work in Jamaica moved her to follow their footsteps. "I wanted to be like them and tell others about Jesus. That is how God called me."[11] Yvette's dream would grow and be grounded in the clear teachings of the Bible and her convictions and confidence in its truth. In her book, *Signs from the Sermon: The Sermon on the Mount for Deaf Readers,* she writes,

> Every person is a sinner. Jesus Christ alone is sinless. The most amazing thing is sinless Jesus BECAME a sinner on the cross, carrying OUR sins. This is no joyful occasion, no day of celebration. Really, it is the most horrible historical event. . . . Why is that so? For a time OUR sins separated Jesus from the holy, loving Father. Any true believer realizes the horror of Sin. The believer shall mourn about his/her sins. But, wait! The prescription is repent. Just as a person previously turned from God in disobedience, so now one can turn to God by humble rejection of SELF and old habits of living for a new life-style. Forgiveness is medicine for a contrite heart. True peace is contentment. And, this is a reality, that every person—sinner or Christian—face the consequences of his or her sins.
>
> Wow, the wonderful life is the Christian repenting of his/her sins and grieving about the evil on earth, then he/she receives the Lord's forgiveness and peace within self.[12]

Yvette is grateful for "hearing churches" even though they often struggle in relating to those who are deaf.[13] After all, she was saved in one. Her spirit of thankfulness is also a model for us. She continues to holds a deep gratitude to God for the IMB, the Southern Baptist Convention, and the Southern Baptist Conference of the Deaf for supporting her.[14] Still, the hearing are not always as sensitive and understanding with the deaf as they could be. If those of us who hear are not careful, we can come across as condescending and superior to our deaf friends. Also, because signing is physically and emotionally draining, a great deal of understanding is often lost. Yvette's story, unfortunately, is a sad commentary on this reality.

After answering the call to missions, Yvette inquired with the IMB (then FMB) about becoming a missionary. Armed with a list of prerequisites, she checked the list and noted that she needed a seminary degree and two years of work experience to qualify. She followed their instructions and enrolled in Southwestern Baptist Theological Seminary. Admitted, she requested American Sign Language interpreters, but the seminary could not afford signers. Thankfully, one student knew some sign language and signed what he could, and fellow students took notes for her. The following year, two new students who were skilled at interpreting volunteered their hours to interpret all her classes until she graduated. After graduating from seminary, Yvette applied for missionary service with the IMB in 1985 only to be turned down because she was "handicapped."[15] She was shocked and confused.[16] It was a dark time in her life. There were no deaf teams or strategies at the IMB at that time. But Yvette did not give up. She patiently waited on the Lord, and the IMB eliminated deafness as a handicap in 1987. She was appointed with a "special assignment" because of her deafness. As Vesta Sauter notes, "She never complained. She trusted the Lord, kept working and kept hoping!"[17]

Today, Yvette is a graduate of Lexington School for the Deaf and holds a bachelor's degree in English and visual arts, a master of education in deaf education, and a master of religious education. Yvette has seen God be faithful all her life: "The Father has always been faithful! I am a Deaf, Black woman. That is my life. This is how my Father made me and sees me. And He sees us like He sees His beloved Son! In the Bible, God says of Jesus, 'You are My beloved Son and with you, I am well-pleased.' It is a blessing and encouragement to know the Father looks at me and says, "You are My beloved daughter! I am also well pleased with you."[18]

Such a God can indeed be trusted in the fullest measure.

Know the Lord Intimately

(PROVERBS 3:6)

Being wise in our own eyes "is the root of foolishness going all the way back to the garden of Eden."[19] Wisdom says, "Trust in the LORD" (3:5). Wisdom says, "know" the Lord "in all your ways" (v. 6). The ESV translates "know" as "acknowledge," but the *CSB* translation "know" is best. It reflects a close, personal, intimate knowledge of our heavenly Father. It is a knowledge that leads to "absolute obedience and surrender in every realm of life."[20] Such knowledge and obedience are rewarded as our Lord guides our way ("will make [our] paths straight") contrary to the crooked and destructive path of the foolish and wicked. Yvette's intimate devotion to her heavenly Father was rewarded despite the many obstacles she faced.

Yvette was appointed with a "special assignment" to Trinidad on December 30, 1989. She was the first deaf missionary ever to be appointed in the history of the mission board. In 1993, she received career appointment as a church associate developer for the deaf in Trinidad. In 2009, the IMB formed the Deaf Affinity as a specific affinity group to be reached with the gospel. The World Federation of the Deaf estimates that there are more than seventy million deaf persons in the world, using more than three hundred different sign languages.[21] Most people are unreached with little or no access to the gospel. And although an international sign language is used informally and at international meetings, it has significant limitations.[22] Research reveals that in the U.S. alone, there are only fifty-eight deaf churches in the SBC for at least three million people, and 40 percent are without a pastor. One hundred major cities are without a single deaf church.[23] The situation is worse globally. More than fifteen hundred deaf people die daily without Jesus.[24] Again, most are unreached and do not know Jesus, even in America. Most have never had the gospel signed to them. "Often ignored and oppressed, the Deaf are some of the least evangelized people on earth."[25] Such a reality compelled Yvette to go.

At the time of her appointment in 1990, Yvette said, "Often I ask God: 'What is so special about me? Why me?' I am simply delighted to reach other people of like language and experiences. The Deaf world is a small world, and I already feel a bond with the Deaf people of Trinidad."[26] Putting this in perspective, Yvette says, "It is all about obedience. We simply should obey Jesus. Turn things over to the Lord. Be submissive. Get trained. Be discipled. Be willing to do what He wants. There are many different mission fields. Be willing to go and work."[27] Listen to a sister in Christ about trusting the Lord fully. Listen to the heart of one who knows the Lord intimately.

Fear the Lord Completely

(PROVERBS 3:7–8)

In our fallen state, we continually face monstrous temptations called pride and self-sufficiency, the foolish ideas that we are our own best advisor and counselor. Lady Wisdom in Proverbs warns us of the folly of this path. She sternly admonishes us, "Don't be wise in your eyes" (v. 7). *The Message* paraphrase reads, "Don't assume that you know it all." In stark contrast to this foolishness we are told, "Fear the LORD and turn away from evil." "Fear the Lord" connotes the idea that we are to revere in holy awe the Lord who is awesome, holy, and majestic. John Piper beautifully ties the fear of the Lord to the cross. He writes, "Jesus died for us to provide a place where we could enjoy the majesty of God with a kind of fear and trembling and reverence and awe, but not a cowering fear."[28] The wonderful result of this fear is we cannot help but "turn away from evil." Fearing the Lord and running toward evil at the same time is impossible. To say it another way, to love the Lord is to hate evil.

Fearing the Lord and running from evil are always wise companions. They are always beneficial as well. Allen Ross writes, "Compliance with this instruction is therapeutic."[29] "This will be healing for your body and strengthening [ESV, "refreshment;" marg. reading "medicine"] for your bones" (v. 8). Spiritually and physically, we will be invigorated. We will flourish.

Yvette arrived in Trinidad in March 1990 as the first deaf person ever sent by the IMB as a missionary. Through the 1990s she served in Trinidad and St. Lucia.[30] She immediately served even though it was a new experience. Yvette trusted the Lord and was faithful. However, the work was often difficult and challenging on a personal level. She was often lonely.[31] During this time Yvette received loving and helpful counseling. She shares, "After one counseling session I just sobbed in the bathroom. The next time I just opened my heart. No reason to hide. God used that to minister to me. I learned to share and be vulnerable. God gave me the grace of perseverance."[32] She faithfully continued in her missionary work until the Lord brought her elsewhere.

In 2002, the Lord opened the door for Yvette to go to Thailand. She would work with the deaf throughout Southeast Asia but especially in Bangkok. Her philosophy as she moved from people group to people group is instructive: "I worked hard to learn about the different cultures. We must adapt while sharing Christ. We must take on their culture and language without their religion in order to bring Christ into their world. Just like Paul! Following Jesus, I determined I would go to places where people don't know Him, wear their clothes, eat their food, stay in their homes, and live as they do and bring the good news."[33] Yvette adopted their culture and gave them Christ.

Going to Thailand was difficult for Yvette though. Culture shock hit hard. She had to learn new sign languages, and she felt very much alone.[34] She struggled spiritually and physically with discouragement.[35] But God sustained her during these difficult times through his saints. She received member-care counseling to deal with panic attacks and culture shock. She received the kindness of friends and colleagues. And she was encouraged by Mary A. Kassian's book *In My Father's House*, which Yvette read and worked through daily.[36] She dealt with one thing at a time and continued to persevere.

Yvette served in Thailand for thirteen years. Jesus continually brought spiritual healing and refreshment into her life (Prov. 3:8) as she walked with him and shared the gospel with others. Yvette ministered to all ages in a deaf school using the stories of the Bible. Storytelling is a part of deaf culture, and she loved using this method to teach her people. While in Thailand, a nineteen-year-old girl began attending. She came from a Buddhist family. Over time Yvette would talk about the Bible with her.[37] Later she started attending the deaf Thai congregation that met in Yvette's living room. By the fourth Sunday, the girl decided to follow Jesus. When she made the decision, the other Thai believers poured their testimonies into her soul. One believer prayed for her, and another baptized her. Yvette continued to disciple her.

One day, the young girl came to Yvette with her eyes shining. When she told Yvette that she liked a boy, Yvette eventually corralled them to tell Bible stories and give instructions concerning marriage. She was not going to leave that to chance even if they did not get serious for marriage. Eventually, they married in Yvette's home, would go on to build a Christian home, and work in Bible translation. Yvette poured her life into those she was ministering to and depended on the stories of Scriptures to disciple them.

Yvette Aarons served with the IMB for twenty-eight years (1989–2016). She continues to serve the Lord from her home in Brooklyn, New York, and remains thankful to everyone who has supported her:

> God, I am grateful and contented to be Yours.
>
> IMB, I am thankful and gratified that you took me on.
>
> Southern Baptists, everywhere including the Southern Baptist Convention and The Southern Baptist Conference of the Deaf: I am in deep gratitude to each one for believing in me and supporting me through a stable salary, top-notch training as given at the time, and persistent prayer.

Summarizing her service to King Jesus, the IMB says of this choice servant, "Yvette retired in January 2016, but her tireless efforts allowed her to cross many bridges in Jesus's name. As a result of Yvette's willingness to obey the call of God on her life, many deaf people from all tribes, peoples and languages will one day join in worship before the throne."[38] What's more, there are more than 200 sign languages with no Bible.[39]

Conclusion

There are more than seventy million deaf persons in the world, and many live among unreached people groups.[40] They have little or no access to the gospel that saves. We need more who are hearing the Savior's call to go to this massive people group who need king Jesus. At the time of this writing, the IMB has less than fifteen people assigned to the Deaf Affinity people group.[41] We could use three hundred, right now, who are willing and ready to go.

Yvette Aarons was and is a trailblazer in mission work to the deaf. She made it possible for others to follow in her footsteps. Vesta Sauter says, "Yvette helped revolutionize many strategies and approaches of the IMB. Sadly, we were not deaf friendly back then. And we are still learning. Yvette was willing to be the first one up. She put up with our ignorance! Yvette was pivotal in training others and is still helping to get deaf translations into the heart languages of others. She has been a massive influence in Deaf missions. Yvette is the Deaf's Lottie Moon and Bertha Smith. She is serious about the things of God. She is direct because these things matter."[42]

Yvette trusted God even when she may not have understood why she was deaf. Instead of elevating what she thought was best, her heart leaned on God. She rested in the truth that he knows what he is doing and that what he is doing is good! Her perspective in all of this has been: "Being deaf is a great asset. The bridge is already built because of my Deafness. I will just need to cross it and reach the Deaf for Jesus."[43] She believes the need among the lost compels Christians to go: "We must go because the lost are everywhere in all kinds of cultures. We go because we have what they don't have. Jesus. Even for me there are no limits. Jesus loves me. He is always with me. Totally undeserved. Like all of us. Take the step. He will take care of you."[44] Yvette Aarons indeed has crossed that bridge to go to the lost. What bridge is God calling you to cross that the gospel might go forth among the nations?

To learn more about Yvette's story or how to better serve the Deaf Christian community, contact gracesoa@ymail.com.

God's Power Made Perfect in Weakness–Put on Glorious Display in the Life of

Lilias Trotter

2 CORINTHIANS 12:7–10

"Oh we are slow to see that it is only our weakness that He needs."[1] This was the heartbeat of a single woman by the name of Lilias Trotter (1853–1928).[2] Born into significant wealth in England, she would be influenced by Hannah Whitall Smith and D. L. Moody, embrace Keswick teachings and a theology of total surrender to Christ, and leave the comforts of England to spend her life in the North African country of Algeria. Because Lilias was afflicted with heart issues most of her life, she was rejected by two mission boards for health reasons.[3] Nevertheless, in the power of Christ and for the sake of Christ, she would go and be spent for her beloved Savior. She would exemplify the truth of 2 Corinthians 12:7–10 that God's power is made perfect through weakness and that we are made strong in our Lord Jesus Christ when we are weak in ourselves. Lilias, describing her arrival to the mission field, knew her weaknesses and need for God's strength:

> On March 9th, 1888, we steamed into the Bay of Algiers, the water below shimmering with phosphorescence, the crescent of the shore set with gleaming lights, and the glorious southern sky above full of its quiet stars. . . . Three of us stood there, looking at our battle-field, none of us fit to pass a doctor for any [mission] society, not knowing a soul in the place, or a sentence of Arabic, or a clue for beginning work on untouched ground; we only knew we had to come. Truly if God needed weakness, He had it! [4]

Second Corinthians 12:1–10 is the heart of the third major section of 2 Corinthians (chap. 10–13). Paul is confronting and countering so-called "super apostles" (11:5), who are really just "false apostles" (11:13). These false apostles reveal themselves as such by boasting in what they have done (11:12–13, 17–18), preaching a false gospel (11:4), and misrepresenting what the true spiritual life is (12:7–10). Genuine spirituality is not found in boasting and bragging about who we are, where we have been, and what we have done. No, true spirituality is found in humility, suffering, and weakness. True spirituality is found in following the example of Christ. Only when we are weak in ourselves can we be strong in Christ. Few people show us this truth better than Isabella Lilias (Lily) Trotter. Two truths from 2 Corinthians are on display in the life of this superlative servant of our Savior.

Life's Challenges Drive Us to the Wisdom of Divine Dependency

(2 CORINTHIANS 12:7–9)

Paul has recounted his vision when he was "caught up to the third heaven" (12:2), "caught up into paradise" (12:4), caught up into the presence of God. He saw and heard things so incredible he cannot even speak of them (12:4). He recognized the danger of pride in such an experience, and so does God. Paul's greatest spiritual lesson in life and ministry will not come by a brief visit to the throne of heaven but by a permanent visitation from a "thorn in the flesh" (v. 7). Paul's thorn drove him to the wisdom of complete and total dependency on God. Lilias Trotter puts it like this: "It is when we come to self-despair, when we feel ourselves locked in, waiting our doom, that the glory and beauty of God's way of escape dawns upon us, and we submit ourselves to Him in it."[5] Paul develops four aspects of this wisdom of divine dependency.

See God's Purpose (12:7)

God hates pride (Prov. 8:13; 16:5), and he has his ways of dealing with it for our good. Paul writes in verse 7, "So that I would not exalt myself, a thorn in the flesh was given to me, a messenger of Satan to torment me so that I would not exalt myself." God used a messenger of Satan to accomplish his good purpose in the life of Paul, perhaps as he did with Job. Paul describes this harassing, bothersome messenger of Satan as a "thorn in the flesh." He was continually tormented by this thorn that God could keep him humble. This adversary was God's tool for Paul's good. We do not know exactly what the thorn was. Scholars have proposed numerous possibilities.[6] One possibility is some type of eye ailment because of Paul's words in Galatians 4:15 and 6:11. We may not know *what* it is, but we do know *why* God gave it.

Lilias Trotter had her own thorns given by God to draw her near in absolute dependence on her heavenly Father. Lilias was born into a wealthy family on July 14, 1853, in London, England. She loved her father only to be devastated by his death when she was twelve. However, his death would cause Lilias to seek a heavenly Father who would be her beloved for the rest of her life.[7] Lilias would be converted, or at least committed, to total surrender, through the Keswick Movement and its emphasis on the victorious Christian life.[8] This would lead to her ministering to prostitutes on the streets of London and, eventually, the mission field of Algeria. In May 1887, a missionary named Edward Glenny of the North African Mission was leading a missionary meeting in London. He asked with a passionate voice, "Is there anyone in this room whom God is calling to North Africa?" Lilias Trotter rose and said, "He is calling me."[9] And the thorn? As she ministered to needy girls and women in London and sought to balance her promising career as an artist, she had a physical breakdown due to exhaustion. She would require an extended period of rest, minor surgery, and suffer permanent damage to her heart, a "thorn" she would endure the rest of her life requiring repeated and extended periods of rest and recuperation.[10]

Lilias's heart condition would cause her to be rejected by the North African Mission twice. But the thorn of poor health did not deter her. She would go to Algeria. From her diary we read of her faith in God's purpose that led her to go: "I am seeing more and more that we begin to learn what it is to walk by faith when we learn to spread out all that is against us: all our physical weaknesses, loss of mental power, spiritual inability—all that is against us inwardly and outwardly—as sailed to the wind and expect them to be vehicles for the power of Christ to rest upon us. It is so simple and self-evident—but so long in the learning!"[11] We must see God's purposes, especially in the "thorns" he brings into our lives.

Seek God in Prayer (12:8)

The thorn kept Paul from pride and drove him to prayer. Paul followed the example of the Lord Jesus in the garden of Gethsemane (Matt 26:36–44) and pleaded with the Lord three times that the thorn in the flesh would leave him (v. 8). Paul's thorn was debilitating and humiliating. It continually knocked him down and showed his weakness. It also drove him to his knees to God.

Likewise, Lilias knew the great need of prayer, and she knew the strength the child of God finds on her knees. She writes,

- "The place where we wash His feet with our tears has a great nearness to His holy place above."
- "Turn full your soul's vision to Jesus, and look at Him, and a strange dimness will come over all that is apart from Him, and the Divine [attraction] by which God's saints are made . . . will lay hold of you. For 'He is worthy' to have all there is to be had in the heart that He died to win."
- "I am beginning to see that it is out of a low place that one can best believe."
- "More and more one sees that prayer is a quiet time for thinking out God's thoughts with Him and giving our 'Amen' in the Name of Jesus."[12]

Submit to God's Plan (12:9)

God revealed his plan to *Paul* through prayer, not in paradise. The answer he received is not what he wanted, but it was what he needed. God's response to his plea to be delivered from "the thorn" is verse 9: "But he [Christ] said to me, 'My grace is sufficient for you, for my power is perfected in weakness.'" Here is the summit of Paul's argument and the heart of what theologians call a "weakness Christology." God's grace and power are supremely revealed in a beaten man on a bloody Roman cross. As it went with Christ, so it goes for us. God's grace and power are put on greatest display when we, too, are weak and small, not strong and great.

This magnificent truth appears in Lilias Trotter's life in the context of her great gift as an artist. Lilias displayed a talent for drawing and painting at an early age. It was natural. She had no formal training. As providence would have it, she met John Ruskin, the most renowned art critic in all of Europe in October 1876. He was smitten both by Lilias as a person and by her art.[13] So taken was he by her that he claimed she changed his mind about women painters. He would write: "For a long time I used to say, in all my elementary books, that, except in a graceful and minor way, women could not paint or draw. I am beginning lately, to bow myself to the much more delightful conviction that no one else can."[14] Of Lilias's natural artistic ability, Ruskin said, "She seemed to learn everything the instant she was shown, and ever so much more than she was taught."[15]

Ruskin was convinced she could develop into one of the greatest artists in all of Europe. In a letter to Blanche Pigott, Lilias writes that Ruskin said if she would give herself completely to this gift, "she would be the greatest living painter and do things that would be Immortal."[16] This brought a crisis and a decision of no return in Lilias's life: choose a career as an artist or choose Christ? Ruskin pressed her. How would she respond to such a storm in her life?

In May 1879 her decision was made. Christ and his kingdom's work must come first. Of this choice of destiny she writes, "I see as clear as daylight now, I cannot give myself to painting in the way he [Ruskin] means and continue still to 'seek first the kingdom of God and His righteous.'"[17] Later, in *Parables of the Cross,* she adds, "The one thing is to keep obedient in spirit. . . . It is loss to keep when God says 'give' . . . [an] independence is the characteristic of the new flood of resurrection life that comes to our souls as we learn this fresh lesson of dying—a grand independence of any earthly thing to satisfy our soul, the liberty of those who have nothing to lose, because they have nothing to keep. We can do without *anything* while we have God. Hallelujah!"[18]

Lilias walked away from this promising art career. She returned to London and gave herself completely to the work God had given her. However, the comforts of Great Britain were not what her Master had for her in the future. North Africa would be both her calling and her final resting place. This was God's plan and one she would faithfully submit to:

> Shall we not ask God to convict us, as to where lies the hindrance to this self-emptying? It is not alone mere selfishness, in its ordinary sense, that prevents it; long after this has been cleansed away by the Precious Blood there may remain, unrecognized, the self-life in more subtle forms. It may co-exist with much that looks like sacrifice; there may be much of usefulness and of outward self-denial, and yet below the surface may remain a clinging to our own judgment, a confidence in our own resources, an

> unconscious taking of our own way, even in God's service. And these things hold down, hold *in* our souls, and frustrate the Spirit in His working. The latent self-life needs to be brought down into the place of death before His breath can carry us hither and thither as the wind wafts the seeds. Are we ready for this last surrender?[19]

Lilias was indeed ready for this last surrender, and she would never look back.

Speak of God's Power (12:9)

God's grace is sufficient. His power is made perfect in weakness. Paul's response is clear-cut: "Therefore, I will most gladly boast [5x in 12:1–9] all the more about my weaknesses, so that Christ's power may reside [ESV, "rest"] in me." The word *reside* carries the idea of "pitch his tent" or "tabernacle." Paul is learning the "divine power in human weakness principle." The omnipotent all-sufficient Savior comes down in power on his people in their need and in their weakness.

Lilias would take the truth of 2 Corinthians 12:9–10 and develop it in her theology and understanding of the crucified life. Death to self is the way of spiritual life and supernatural power. Her classic *Parables of the Cross* guides us into the heart and mind of this remarkable servant of Christ.

> Put the Cross of Christ, in its mysterious delivering power, *irrevocably* between you and sinning, and hold on there. That is your part, and you must do it. There is no further progress possible to you, till you make up your mind to part company with every sin in which you know you are indulging—every sin of

thought, word, or deed, every link with the world, the flesh, or the devil, everything on which the shadow of a question falls, as God's light shines in: to part company, not by a series of gradual struggles, but by an honest act of renouncing, maintained by faith and obedience. And as you make the decision up to present knowledge, you must determine that this is henceforth your attitude towards *all* that is "not of the Father," as His growing light shall reveal it.[20] . . .

Yes, there lies before us a beautiful *possible* life—one that shall have a passion for giving: that shall be poured forth to God—spent out for man: that shall be consecrated "for the hardest work and the darkest sinners." But how are we to enter in? How are we to escape from the self-life that holds us, even after the sin-life has loosed its grasp? Back to the Cross: not only from the world of condemnation and from the world of sinning does it free us as we accept it, but from the power of outward things and from the thraldom of self: not only does it open the door into the world of acquittal, and again into that of holiness, but yet again into the new realm of surrender, and thence into that of sacrifice. For the essential idea of the Cross is a life lost to be found again in those around.[21] . . . Are our hands off the very blossom of our life? Are all things—even the treasures that He has sanctified—held loosely, ready to be parted with, without a struggle, when He asks for them?[22] . . .

A dying must come upon *all* that would hinder God's working through us—all interest, all impulses,

> all energies that are "born of the flesh"—all that is merely human, and apart from His Spirit. Only thus can the Life of Jesus, in its intensity of love for sinners, have its way in our souls.[23]

Supernatural Sufficiency Drives Us to the Wisdom of Personal Humility

(2 CORINTHIANS 12:10)

When we empty ourselves of self, God can then fill us with himself. However, this supernatural filling may not look like you would think. Nevertheless, a strange and paradoxical contentment is the gift our God grants us. Such a promise motivated Lilias to go to those who had never heard the name of Jesus. She would write, "How the angels must watch the first day that light reaches a new spot on this earth that God so loves . . . and oh the joy of being allowed to go with His message that first day. How can His people hold back from that joy while one corner remains unvisited by the Dayspring!"[24]

Lilias knew well the opposition and suffering that awaited her even as the angels in heaven rejoiced. She would be humbled and humiliated. But it was all "for the sake of Christ," and he would show himself sufficient in Algeria till the day of her death.

We Serve for Christ's Sake

"For the sake of Christ," Paul says he is content (CSB, "take pleasure"; NIV, "delight"). But where exactly does he find contentment? The answer is amazing. It is in five things: "weaknesses, insults, hardships, persecutions, and in difficulties [ESV, "calamities"]." Paul already provided a list of hardships in 11:23–29. This list in 12:10 is more of a summary. However, the key that unlocks both lists is the same: "For the sake of Christ." It is not about us. It is all about him. As Jim Elliot says, "We are just a bunch of nobodies trying to exalt somebody."[25] If we suffer to make much of Him, we can take pleasure.

This philosophy of life could be written over the mission ministry of Lilias Trotter. Upon her arrival in Algeria, she immediately immersed herself in her work and the culture. She had to learn the language from scratch. She kept detailed diaries and would give herself to a prolific ministry of writing. This would include letters, gospel tracts, evangelistic parables, journal articles, devotional materials, and books.[26]

The first years in Algeria were filled with hardships. Lilias described it as "knocking our heads against stone walls."[27] A close friend summarized the first five years as "unmitigated anguish."[28] After seventeen years on the field, there were few converts and only one new woman missionary had permanently joined the work.[29] Reflecting on her trials and challenges, Lilias would write in the context of the Lord's Supper:

> His true cup with all its infirmity of meaning is ours to have and hold. The cup of sacrifice to the uttermost . . . shall we dare take from the Lord's Hands the cup of fellowship over these lands that He loves? It may mean a transforming of our lives: for the passion of caring, the passion of prayer, the passion of giving that are in Him cannot come into our hearts without somewhere burning their way through. Well may He ask, 'Are ye able?'"[30]

Here is a woman who clearly knew what "weaknesses, insults, hardships, persecutions, and difficulties" looked like year after year on the mission field and braved them all for Christ's sake.

We Serve in Christ's Strength

After mentioning various forms of hardship, Paul's finishing declaration is resounding. He can say he is content in such difficulties because "when I am weak, then I am strong" (v. 10), How is this so? How is it possible to consider ourselves occupying the strongest position in the moment we feel most feeble? It is possible because when we are weak, God tabernacles over us. When we are weak, *his* grace pours over us. When we are weak, *he* is strong for us. When we are weak, *he* does *his* perfect work. Paul had come to see God does his best work in our weakness! There supernatural strength in Christ is discovered, a power that will sustain us day by day until our race is finished.

Lilias Trotter went through seasons where she felt she had failed. However, God sustained her, and the fruit would come. Eventually, the work in Algeria grew. Bible studies and prayer groups for women sprang up. Lilias and her companions taught new believers the Bible and principles of leadership. Rebecca Pate writes, "Eventually, they established mission stations in several parts of Algeria from the Mediterranean to the mountains. The desire to see North Africans come to Christ eventually led Trotter to begin an itineration ministry into the Sahara in both Algeria and Tunisia, particularly to visit the Sufi brotherhood, a group of Muslim mystics. [The women] considered their trips into the desert extremely important as their sole purpose was to bring the gospel to those who had not heard it."[31]

In 1905, when Lilias was fifty-two years old, after living in the Muslim neighborhoods of the Algiers city center for years, the women purchased an old Turkish palace outside the city, naming it Dar Naama, meaning "house of grace." And "for the next six decades, Dar Naama became the center of the AMB's work," serving missionaries, new recruits, and national believers.[32] After

Lilias's death, her friend Constance Padwick would write this: "'She was the greatest missionary in North African Missions' said a French fellow missionary to the present writer, but it was an unconscious greatness, for like the children 'of whom is the Kingdom of heaven' or the scientist or the artist that she was by nature and endowment, Lilias Trotter's habit of mind was one of an intense, self-forgetting, reverent and delighted absorption in God's world and His ways whether in outward beauty or in the spiritual drama."[33]

Samuel Zwemer, the "apostle to Islam" would say this of Lilias: "My best impression of her life could best be expressed in two words—it was a life of Vision and a life of Prayer. Her eyes seemed ever looking upward, and also gazed below the surface of things. She was indiscourageable in happiness and steadfast in faith, and was an embodiment of her own expression, 'The Glory of the Impossible.' Personally, I owe very much to her missionary messages, which were my inspiration and comfort in the early days of my pioneering work in Arabia."[34]

Biographer Miriam Rockness adds: "Lilias left a vigorous legacy in the work itself. The Algiers Mission Band was on solid footing when she died, thirty members strong in fifteen stations and outposts, unified in mission and purpose. She pioneered missionary methods and approaches to evangelism for which noted missiologist Dr. Christy Wilson called her 'one hundred years ahead of her time.'"[35]

Conclusion

Lilias Trotter was bed-ridden the last years of her earthly life. She continued to serve the cause of missions, especially through the ministry of prayer. She died in her bed on August 27, 1928, in

Dar Naama, Algeria. She was seventy-six. As she neared her death and those who loved her gathered around her bed singing her favorite hymn "Jesus Lover of My Soul," she exclaimed, "A chariot and six horses." Her friend Helen Freeman responded, "You are seeing many beautiful things?" Lilias looked up and spoke her final words, "Yes, many, many beautiful things." She then lifted her hands in prayer, breathed her final breath, and made her way home to the "Lover of her soul," King Jesus.[36]

Lilias (Lalla Lili as she was called by the Algerians who so loved her), was laid to rest in the North African country of Algeria she loved and served for four decades.[37] The song that inspired her throughout her life, penned by the wonderful hymnwriter Charles Wesley, closes our study of this precious and faithful saint who shows us the wonderful truth: Christ's power is made perfect in weakness.

> Jesus, lover of my soul, Let me to Thy bosom fly,
> While the nearer waters roll, While the tempest still is high:
> Hide me, O my Savior, hide, Till the storm of life is past;
> Safe into the haven guide; O receive my soul at last.
>
> Other refuge have I none; Hangs my helpless soul on Thee;
> Leave, O leave me not alone, Still support and comfort me:
> All my trust on Thee is stayed, All my help from Thee I bring;
> Cover my defenseless head, With the shadow of Thy wing.

Thou, O Christ, art all I want; More than all in
Thee I find:
Raise the fallen, cheer the faint, Heal the sick, and
lead the blind:
Just and holy is Thy name, I am all
unrighteousness;
False and full of sin I am, Thou art full of truth
and grace.

Plenteous grace with Thee is found, Grace to cover
all my sin;
Let the healing streams abound; Make and keep me
pure within:
Thou of life the fountain art, Freely let me take of
Thee;
Spring Thou up within my heart; Rise to all
eternity.[38]

Works Cited

Anderson, Courtney. *To the Golden Shore: The Life of Adoniram Judson*. Valley Forge: Judson Press, 1987.

Andrew, John A. "Betsey Stockton: Stranger in a Strange Land." *Journal of Presbyterian History (1962–1985)* 52, no. 2 (1974): 157–66.

Barrett, Ken. "Baptist Church Restoration a Mixed Blessing for Myanmar." *Nikkei Asian Review*, December 24, 2017. https://asia.nikkei.com/Life-Arts/Life/Baptist-church-restoration-a-mixed-blessing-for-Myanmar2.

Beck, Rosalie. "More than Rubies." *Christian History Institute.* Accessed January 16, 2020. https://christianhistoryinstitute.org/magazine/article/more-than-rubies.

Boice, James Montgomery. *Psalms: Psalms 107–150.* Vol. 3. Grand Rapids, MI: Baker, 2005.

Brown, Arthur Judson. *The Lien-Chou Martyrdom: The Cross Is Still Upheld at Lien-Chou*. New York, NY: Board of Foreign Missions of the Presbyterian Church in the United States of America, 1906.

Brown, G. Thompson. "Eleanor Chestnut." *Biographical Dictionary of Christian Missions*. Edited by Gerald H. Anderson. New York: Macmillan, 1998.

Burrage, Henry S. *Baptist Hymn Writers and Their Hymns.* Portland, ME: Brown Thurston & Co., 1888.

Carson, D. A. *The Gospel according to John*. Grand Rapids, MI: Eerdmans, 1990.

Chambers, Oswald. *My Utmost for His Highest*. Westwood, NJ: Discovery House, 1963.

Cowart, John. *Strangers on the Earth*. Bluefish Books, 2006.

Drummond, Lewis. *Miss Bertha: Woman of Revival: A Biography*. Nashville, TN: B&H Publishing Group, 1996.

Elliot, Elisabeth. *A Path through Suffering*. Grand Rapids, MI: Revell, 2003.

———. *Shadow of the Almighty: The Life and Testament of Jim Elliot*. San Francisco, CA: HarperOne, 1956.

Escher, Constance K. *She Calls Herself Betsey Stockton: The Illustrated Odyssey of a Princeton Slave*. Eugene, OR: Resource Publications, 2022.

Forester, Fanny. *Missionary Biography. The Memoir of Sarah B. Judson, Member of the American Mission to Burmah*. London: Aylott & Jones, 1848.

Gardner, Paul D. *1 Corinthians*. Zondervan Exegetical Commentary on the New Testament. Grand Rapids, MI: Zondervan Academic, 2018.

Handy, Wes. "'An Historical Analysis of the North China Mission (SBC) And Keswick Sanctification in the Shandong Revival,' 1927–1937." Wake Forest, NC: Southeastern Baptist Theological Seminary, 2012.

James, Sharon. *Ann Judson: A Missionary Life for Burma*. Darlington, UK: Evangelical Press, 2015.

Jordan, Willie. "Christ-Like Love." Fred Jordan Missions, June 16, 2020. https://www.fjm.org/daily-devotional/christ-like-love.

Keller, Tim. "Galatians: Living in Line with the Truth of the Gospel." *Gospel in Life*. Accessed September 8, 2022. https://gospelinlife.com/downloads/galatians-living-in-line-with-the-truth-of-the-gospel-group-study-product.

Kidner, Derek. *Psalms 1–72*. Tyndale Old Testament Commentaries. Downers Grove, IL: InterVarsity Press, 1973.

———. *Psalms 73–150*. Tyndale Old Testament Commentaries. Downers Grove, IL: InterVarsity Press, 1973.

Kirkland, Don. "Exhibit Honoring 'Miss Bertha' Opens at SBC Library & Archives." *Baptist Press*, February 21, 2005. https://www.baptistpress.com/resource-library/news/exhibit-honoring-miss-bertha-opens-at-sbc-library-archives.

Lewis, C. S. *The Four Loves*. San Francisco, CA: HarperOne, 2017.

Moffett, Eileen F. "Betsey Stockton: Pioneer American Missionary." *International Bulletin of Missionary Research* 19, no. 2 (April 1995): 71.

Morgan, Robert J. *On This Day 365 Amazing and Inspiring Stories about Saints, Martyrs and Heroes*. Nashville: Nelson, 1997.

Morris, Leon. *1 Corinthians*. Revised Edition. Tyndale New Testament Commentaries. Downers Grove, IL: IVP Academic, 1988.

———. *Galatians: Paul's Charter of Christian Freedom*. Downers Grove, IL: InterVarsity Press, 1996.

Motyer, Alec. *Psalms by the Day: A New Devotional Translation*. Fearn, Ross-shire: Christian Focus, 2016.

Newell, Harriet. *Delighting in Her Heavenly Bridegroom: The Memoirs of Harriet Newell, Teenage Missionary Wife*. Edited by Jennifer Adams. Forest, VA: Corner Pillar Press, 2011.

Nobles, Gregory H. *The Education of Betsey Stockton: An Odyssey of Slavery and Freedom*. Chicago: University of Chicago Press, 2022.

Piper, John. "As I Have Loved You, Love One Another." Desiring God, March 17, 2012. https://www.desiringgod.org/messages/as-i-have-loved-you-love-one-another.

———. *Future Grace, Revised Edition: The Purifying Power of the Promises of God*. Revised Edition. Colorado Springs, CO: Multnomah, 2012.

———. "I Do Not Nullify the Grace of God." Desiring God. March 6, 1983. https://www.desiringgod.org/messages/i-do-not-nullify-the-grace-of-god.

———. "Only a New Creation Counts." Desiring God. August 28, 1983. https://www.desiringgod.org/messages/only-a-new-creation-counts.

———. "Your Job as Ministry." Desiring God. June 14, 1981. https://www.desiringgod.org/messages/your-job-as-ministry.

Robert, Dana L. "The Mother of Modern Missions." *Christian History and Biography* 90 (April 1, 2006): 22–24.

Rose, Darlene Deibler. *Evidence Not Seen: A Woman's Miraculous Faith in the Jungles of World War II*. San Francisco, CA: Harper Collins, 1990.

Ross, Allen. *A Commentary on the Psalms: 1–41.* Vol. 1. Grand Rapids, MI: Kregel Academic, 2012.

Ross, Allen P. *A Commentary on the Psalms: 90–150.* Vol. 3. Grand Rapids, MI: Kregel, 2014.

Schreiner, Thomas R. *1 Corinthians: An Introduction and Commentary.* Downers Grove, IL: IVP Academic, 2018.

———. *Galatians.* Zondervan Exegetical Commentary Series vol. 9. Grand Rapids, MI: Zondervan, 2010.

Smith, Bertha. "LETTER FROM CHINA, Bertha Smith: 'Unworthy of the Privilege.'" *Baptist Press,* August 8, 2008. https://www.baptistpress.com/resource-library/news/letter-from-china-bertha-smith-unworthy-of-the-privilege.

Smith, Bertha, Timothy George, and Denise George. *Go Home and Tell.* Library of Baptist Classics Vol. 8. Nashville, TN: Broadman & Holman, 1995.

Speer, Robert E. *Servants of the King.* New York, NY: Young People's Missionary Movement of the United States and Canada, 1909.

Spurgeon, C. H. *The Treasury of David: Psalm 111–150* Vol. 3. Grand Rapids, MI: Zondervan, 1979.

Stevens, Robert J., and Brian Johnson. *Profiles of African-American Missionaries.* Pasadena, CA: William Carey Library, 2012.

Strong, E. S. "Our Martyered Dead." *The Institute Tie,* 1906.

Stuart, Arabella W. *Lives of the Three Mrs. Judsons.* Charleston, SC: BiblioBazar, 2007.

Tucker, Ruth. *From Jerusalem to Irian Jaya: A Biographical History of Christian Missions*. Grand Rapids, MI: Zondervan, 2004.

VanGemeren, Willem A. *Psalms*. Edited by Tremper Longman III and David E. Garland. Revised Edition. *The Expositor's Bible Commentary*. Grand Rapids, MI: Zondervan, 2008.

Vaughan, Curtis. *Galatians: A Study Guide*. Grand Rapids, MI: Zondervan, 1972.

Vaughn, Curtis, and Thomas D. Lea. *1 Corinthians*. Bible Study Commentary. Grand Rapids, MI: Zondervan, 1984.

Verstraete, Susan. "'With Skilled, Kind Fingers That Did Not Tremble': The Story of Dr. Eleanor Chesnut." Bulletin Inserts. Accessed January 5, 2023. https://bulletininserts.org/with-skilled-kind-fingers-that-did-not-tremble-the-story-of-dr-eleanor-chesnut.

Wiersbe, Warren W. *Be Transformed: An Expository Study of John 13–21*. Wheaton, IL: Victor Books, 1986.

———. *Be Wise*. Wheaton, IL: Victor Books, 1987.

"Bertha Smith Legacy." *Baptist Courier*. December 23, 2010. https://baptistcourier.com/2010/12/bertha-smith-legacy.

"Betsey Stockton." *Black Heritage Now*, August 30, 2014. https://blackhistorynow.com/betsey-stockton.

"Letters concerning Chestnut, Eleanor. 1905–1908." Accessed February 14, 2023. http://archive.org/details/lettersconerning00unse_15.

"Myanmar (Burma) | Joshua Project." Accessed January 16, 2020. https://joshuaproject.net/countries/BM.

"Rose, Darlene." *The Chattanoogan*. Chatannooga, TN, February 29, 2004. https://www.chattanoogan.com/2004/2/29/47410/Rose-Darlene.aspx.

"The Man Who Gave the Bible to the Burmese." *Christian History & Biography Magazine*, 2006. Accessed January 24, 2020. https://christianhistoryinstitute.org/magazine/article/the-man-who-gave-the-bible-to-the-burmese.

Notes

Introduction

1. Elisabeth Elliot, *Shadow of the Almighty: The Life and Testament of Jim Elliot* (San Francisco: Harper & Row, 1989), 46.

2. Gregory Thornbury, *Recovering Classic Evangelicalism: Applying the Wisdom and Vision of Carl F. H. Henry* (Wheaton, IL: Crossway, 2013), 175.

Chapter 1

1. This chapter by Daniel L. Akin in its original form can be found in the Christ-Centered Exposition Commentary Series, particularly the volume entitled *Exalting Jesus in Psalms 101–150,* on pages 260–80. Reproduced, slightly adapted (from academic standards to trade standards), and used with permission.

2. Willem A. VanGemeren, *The Expositor's Bible Commentary: Psalms, Proverbs, Ecclesiastes, Song of Songs*, vol. 5 (Grand Rapids, MI: Zondervan, 1991), 955.

3. Henry S. Burrage, *Baptist Hymn Writers and Their Hymns* (Portland, ME: Brown Thurston & Co., 1888), 302. Concerning this hymn's origin, Burrage writes, "By Dr. Hatfield, the well-known hymnologist, this hymn is ascribed to Mrs. Sarah B. Judson, but on what grounds I am not informed."

4. Allen P Ross, *A Commentary on the Psalms 90–150*, vol. 3 (Grand Rapids, MI: Kregel, 2014), 804.

5. C. H. Spurgeon, *The Treasury of David: Psalm 111–150*, vol. 3 (Grand Rapids, MI: Zondervan, 1979), 244–45.

6. Rosalie Beck, "More Than Rubies," *Christian History Institute*, accessed January 16, 2020, https://christianhistoryinstitute.org/magazine/article/more-than-rubies.

7. Fanny Forester, *Missionary Biography. The Memoir of Sarah B. Judson, Member of the American Mission to Burmah* (London: Aylott & Jones, 1848), 11.

8. Arabella W. Stuart, *Lives of the Three Mrs. Judsons* (Charleston, SC: BiblioBazar, 2007), 135.

9. Forester, *Missionary Biography*, 24–25.

10. Forester, *Missionary Biography*, 25–26.

11. Alec Motyer, *Psalms by the Day: A New Devotional Translation* (Fearn, Ross-shire: Christian Focus, 2016), 396.

12. *Forester, Missionary Biography*, 44.

13. Stuart, *Lives of the Three Mrs. Judsons*, 147.

14. Stuart, *Lives of the Three Mrs. Judsons*, 154.

15. Ross, *Psalms 90–150*, 3:806.

16. Spurgeon, *The Treasury of David*, 246.

17. Stuart, *Lives of the Three Mrs. Judsons*, 160.

18. Stuart, *Lives of the Three Mrs. Judsons.*

19. Stuart, *Lives of the Three Mrs. Judsons.*

20. Stuart, *Lives of the Three Mrs. Judsons*, 163.

21. Forester, *Missionary Biography*, 82–83.

22. Stuart, *Lives of the Three Mrs. Judsons*, 86.

23. Forester, *Missionary Biography*, 90.

24. Forester, *Missionary Biography*, 106–7.

25. Forester, *Missionary Biography*, 122.

26. "The Man Who Gave the Bible to the Burmese," *Christian History & Biography Magazine*, 2006, accessed January 24, 2020, https://christianhistoryinstitute.org/magazine/article/the-man-who-gave-the-bible-to-the-burmese.

27. Forester, *Missionary Biography*, 174–75.

28. Forester, *Missionary Biography*, 175–76.

29. Forester, *Missionary Biography*, 177.

30. Forester, *Missionary Biography*, 169–70.

31. "Myanmar (Burma) | Joshua Project," accessed January 16, 2020, https://joshuaproject.net/countries/BM; Ken Barrett, "Baptist Church Restoration a Mixed Blessing for Myanmar," *Nikkei Asian Review*, December 24, 2017, accessed January 16, 2020, https://asia.nikkei.com/Life-Arts/Life/Baptist-church-restoration-a-mixed-blessing-for-Myanmar2.

Chapter 2

1. D. A. Carson, *The Gospel according to John* (Grand Rapids, MI: Eerdmans, 1990), 484–85.

2. Carson, *The Gospel according to John*, 484.

3. Susan Verstraete, "'With Skilled, Kind Fingers That Did Not Tremble': The Story of Dr. Eleanor Chesnut," Bulletin Inserts, n.d., accessed January 5, 2023, https://bulletininserts.org/with-skilled-kind-fingers-that-did-not-tremble-the-story-of-dr-eleanor-chesnut.

4. Verstraete, "With Skilled, Kind Fingers That Did Not Tremble."

5. Verstraete, "With Skilled, Kind Fingers That Did Not Tremble."

6. E. S. Strong, "Our Martyered Dead," *The Institute Tie*, 1906, 258.

7. Verstraete, "With Skilled, Kind Fingers That Did Not Tremble."

8. Verstraete, "With Skilled, Kind Fingers That Did Not Tremble."

9. Warren W. Wiersbe, *Be Transformed: An Expository Study of John 13–21* (Wheaton, IL: Victor Books, 1986), 16.

10. Verstraete, "With Skilled, Kind Fingers That Did Not Tremble."

11. Verstraete, "With Skilled, Kind Fingers That Did Not Tremble."

12. John Cowart, *Strangers on the Earth* (Bluefish Books, 2006), 138.

13. Cowart, *Strangers on the Earth*, 139.

14. G. Thompson Brown, "Elenor Chestnut," in *Biographical Dictionary of Christian Missions*, ed. Gerald H. Anderson (Grand Rapids, MI: Eerdmans, 1999).

15. Robert J. Morgan, *On This Day in Christian History: 365 Amazing and Inspiring Stories about Saints, Martyrs and Heroes* (Nashville: Nelson, 1997).

16. Ruth Tucker, *From Jerusalem to Irian Jaya: A Biographical History of Christian Missions* (Grand Rapids, MI: Zondervan, 2004), 420.

17. *"A Bathroom, A Leg, and $1.50,"* https://tinyurl.com/yw55t52h.

18. Cowart, *Strangers on the Earth*, 141.

19. C. S. Lewis, *The Four Loves* (San Francisco, CA: HarperOne, 2017), 156–57.

20. "Letters Concerning Chestnut, Eleanor. 1905–1908," accessed February 14, 2023, http://archive.org/details/lettersconerning00unse_15.

21. Robert E. Speer, *Servants of the King* (New York: Young People's Missionary Movement of the United States and Canada, 1909), 99.

22. Arthur Judson Brown, *The Lien-Chou Martyrdom: The Cross Is Still Upheld at Lien-Chou* (New York: Board of Foreign Missions of the Presbyterian Church in the United States of America, 1906), 22.

23. Lewis, *The Four Loves*, 155–56.

24. Willie Jordan, "Christ-Like Love," Fred Jordan Missions, June 16, 2020, https://www.fjm.org/daily-devotional/christ-like-love.

25. *Apologeticus* ch. 39, sect. 7.

26. Speer, *Servants of the King*, 109.

27. Brown, *The Lien-Chou Martyrdom*, 10.

28. Brown, *The Lien-Chou Martyrdom*, 25.

29. John Piper, "As I Have Loved You, Love One Another," Desiring God, March 17, 2012, https://www.desiringgod.org/messages/as-i-have-loved-you-love-one-another.

Chapter 3

1. This chapter by Daniel L. Akin in its original form can be found in the Christ-Centered Exposition Commentary Series, particularly the volume entitled *Exalting Jesus in Psalms 101–150*, on pages 305–13. Used with permission.

2. Dana L. Robert, "The Mother of Modern Missions," *Christian History and Biography* 90 (April 1, 2006): 22–24.

3. C. H. Spurgeon, *The Treasury of David: Psalm 111–150*, vol. 3b (Grand Rapids, MI: Zondervan, 1979), 324.

4. Spurgeon, *The Treasury of David*, 324.

5. Sharon James, *Ann Judson: A Missionary Life for Burma* (Darlington, UK: Evangelical Press, 2015), 24–25.

6. James, *Ann Judson*, 33.

7. James, *Ann Judson*, 39–42.

8. Allen P Ross, *A Commentary on the Psalms: 90–150*, vol. 3 (Grand Rapids, MI: Kregel, 2014), 870.

9. James, *Ann Judson*, 191–92.

10. James, *Ann Judson*, 213–14.

11. James Montgomery Boice, *Psalms: Psalms 107–150*, vol. 3 (Grand Rapids, MI: Baker, 2005), 1232–33.

12. Alec Motyer, *Psalms by the Day: A New Devotional Translation* (Fearn, Ross-shire: Christian Focus, 2016), 405.

13. Motyer, *Psalms by the Day*, 405.

14. Courtney Anderson, *To the Golden Shore: The Life of Adoniram Judson* (Valley Forge: Judson Press, 1987), 380–81.

15. Robert, "The Mother of Modern Missions," 24.

16. Robert, "The Mother of Modern Missions," 24.

17. James, *Ann Judson*, 259.

Chapter 4

1. This chapter by Daniel L. Akin can be originally found in the Christ-Centered Exposition Commentary Series, particularly the volume entitled *Exalting Jesus in Psalms 101–150*, on pages 145–57. Reproduced, slightly adapted (from academic standards to trade standards), and used with permission.

2. Elisabeth Elliot, *A Path through Suffering* (Grand Rapids, MI: Revell, 2003), 39.

3. Harriet Newell, *Delighting in Her Heavenly Bridegroom: The Memoirs of Harriet Newell, Teenage Missionary Wife*, ed. Jennifer Adams (Forest, VA: Corner Pillar Press, 2011), 238.

4. Newell, *Delighting in Her Heavenly Bridegroom*, 124.

5. Newell, *Delighting in Her Heavenly Bridegroom*, 75.

6. Newell, *Delighting in Her Heavenly Bridegroom*, 86.

7. Newell, *Delighting in Her Heavenly Bridegroom*, 96.

8. Newell, *Delighting in Her Heavenly Bridegroom*, 85–87.

9. Newell, *Delighting in Her Heavenly Bridegroom*, 98.

10. Newell, *Delighting in Her Heavenly Bridegroom*, 100.

11. Newell, *Delighting in Her Heavenly Bridegroom*, 105.

12. Newell, *Delighting in Her Heavenly Bridegroom*, 214.

13. John Piper, *Future Grace: The Purifying Power of the Promises of God*, Rev. Ed. (Colorado Springs, CO: Multnomah, 2012), xiv.

14. C. H. Spurgeon, *The Treasury of David: Psalm 111–150*, vol. 3b (Grand Rapids, MI: Zondervan, 1979), 70.

15. Newell, *Delighting in Her Heavenly Bridegroom*, 64–65.

16. Newell, *Delighting in Her Heavenly Bridegroom*, 68.

17. Newell, *Delighting in Her Heavenly Bridegroom*, 69.

18. Newell, *Delighting in Her Heavenly Bridegroom*, 124.

19. Oswald Chambers, *My Utmost for His Highest* (Westwood, NJ: Discovery House, 1963).

20. Newell, *Delighting in Her Heavenly Bridegroom*, 203.

21. Newell, *Delighting in Her Heavenly Bridegroom*, 207–11.

22. Derek Kidner, *Psalms 73–150*, Tyndale Old Testament Commentaries (Downers Grove, IL: InterVarsity Press, 1973), 411.

23. Newell, *Delighting in Her Heavenly Bridegroom*, 216.

24. Newell, *Delighting in Her Heavenly Bridegroom*, 238–39.

25. Newell, *Delighting in Her Heavenly Bridegroom*, 209.

26. Newell, *Delighting in Her Heavenly Bridegroom*, 159–60.

27. Newell, *Delighting in Her Heavenly Bridegroom*, 222.

28. Newell, *Delighting in Her Heavenly Bridegroom*, 13.

29. Newell, *Delighting in Her Heavenly Bridegroom*, 237.

30. Newell, *Delighting in Her Heavenly Bridegroom*, 238.

31. For more on Harriett Newell, see: *Delighting in Her Heavenly Bridegroom: The Memoirs of Harrett Newell Teenage Missionary Wife*, edited and annotated by Jennifer Adam.

Chapter 5

1. This chapter by Daniel L. Akin in its original form can be found in the Christ-Centered Exposition Commentary Series, particularly the volume entitled *Exalting Jesus in Psalms 1–50*, on pages 199–211. Reproduced, slightly adapted (from academic standards to trade standards), and used with permission.

2. Darlene Deibler Rose, *Evidence Not Seen: A Woman's Miraculous Faith in the Jungles of World War II* (San Francisco, CA: Harper Collins, 1990), 46.

3. Derek Kidner, *Psalms 1–72*, Tyndale Old Testament Commentaries (Downers Grove, IL: InterVarsity Press, 1973), 117.

4. See Willem A. VanGemeren, *Psalms*, ed. Tremper Longman III and David E. Garland, Rev. Ed., The Expositor's Bible Commentary (Grand Rapids, MI: Zondervan, 2008), 281.

5. Allen Ross, *A Commentary on the Psalms: 1–41*, vol. 1 (Grand Rapids, MI: Kregel Academic, 2012), 621.

6. Rose, *Evidence Not Seen*, 131.

7. Rose, *Evidence Not Seen*, 46.

8. Rose, *Evidence Not Seen*, 135.

9. VanGemeren, *Psalms*, 244.

10. Rose, *Evidence Not Seen*, 109.

11. Rose, *Evidence Not Seen*.

12. Rose, *Evidence Not Seen*, 143.

13. Rose, *Evidence Not Seen*, 111.

14. Rose, *Evidence Not Seen*, 125.

15. Michael Altenburg, "Fear Not, O Little Flock, the Foe," public domain.

16. Rose, *Evidence Not Seen*, 126.

17. Rose, *Evidence Not Seen*, 137.

18. Rose, *Evidence Not Seen*, 141.

19. Rose, *Evidence Not Seen*.

20. This hymn has a 1941 copyright, renewed in 1969. https://hymnary.org/text/he_giveth_more_grace_as_our_burdens.

21. Rose, *Evidence Not Seen*, 141–42.

22. Rose, *Evidence Not Seen*, 148–50.

23. Rose, *Evidence Not Seen*, 142.

24. Rose, *Evidence Not Seen*, 154–55.

25. "Rose, Darlene," The Chattanoogan (Chatannooga, TN, February 29, 2004), https://www.chattanoogan.com/2004/2/29/47410/Rose-Darlene.aspx.

26. Rose, *Evidence Not Seen*, 224.

27. Rose, *Evidence Not Seen*, 47.

Chapter 6

1. John Piper, "Your Job as Ministry," *Desiring God*, June 14, 1981, https://www.desiringgod.org/messages/your-job-as-ministry.

2. Constance K. Escher, *She Calls Herself Betsey Stockton: The Illustrated Odyssey of a Princeton Slave* (Eugene, OR: Resource Publications, 2022), 18.

3. Eileen F. Moffett, "Betsey Stockton: Pioneer American Missionary," *International Bulletin of Missionary Research* 19, no. 2 (April 1995): 72.

4. Moffett, "Betsey Stockton."

5. Curtis Vaughn and Thomas D. Lea, *1 Corinthians*, Bible Study Commentary (Grand Rapids, MI: Zondervan, 1984), 77.

6. Paul D. Gardner, *1 Corinthians*, Zondervan Exegetical Commentary on the New Testament (Grand Rapids, MI: Zondervan Academic, 2018), 326.

7. Thomas R. Schreiner, *1 Corinthians: An Introduction and Commentary* (Downers Grove, IL: IVP Academic, 2018), 148–49.

8. Schreiner, *1 Corinthians*, 150–51.

9. Leon Morris, *1 Corinthians*, Rev. Ed., Tyndale New Testament Commentaries (Downers Grove, IL: IVP Academic, 1988), 110–11.

10. Escher, *She Calls Herself Betsey Stockton*, 18.

11. Escher, *She Calls Herself Betsey Stockton*, 18–19.

12. Warren W. Wiersbe, *Be Wise* (Wheaton, IL: Victor Books, 1987), 86.

13. Moffett, "Betsey Stockton," 72.

14. Escher, *She Calls Herself Betsey Stockton*, 22–23.

15. Escher, *She Calls Herself Betsey Stockton*, 24.

16. Escher, *She Calls Herself Betsey Stockton*, 34–86.

17. John A. Andrew, "Betsey Stockton: Stranger in a Strange Land," *Journal of Presbyterian History (1962–1985)* 52, no. 2 (1974): 163.

18. "Betsey Stockton," *Black Heritage Now*, August 30, 2014, accessed January 4, 2023, https://blackhistorynow.com/betsey-stockton.

19. Gregory H. Nobles, *The Education of Betsey Stockton: An Odyssey of Slavery and Freedom* (Chicago: The University of Chicago Press, 2022), 147.

20. Moffett, "Betsey Stockton," 74.

21. Robert J. Stevens and Brian Johnson, *Profiles of African-American Missionaries* (Pasadena, CA: William Carey Library, 2012), 72.

22. Moffett, "Betsey Stockton," 74. The previous sentence's information about Lewis Mudge is also taken from this source.

23. Nobles, *The Education of Betsey Stockton*, 220.

24. Nobles, *The Education of Betsey Stockton*, 220.

25. Nobles, *The Education of Betsey Stockton*, 221.

Chapter 7

1. Bertha Smith, Timothy George, and Denise George, *Go Home and Tell*, Library of Baptist Classics, vol. 8 (Nashville, TN: Broadman & Holman, 1995), 11.

2. Smith, George, and George, *Go Home and Tell*, 215–16.

3. Smith, George, and George, *Go Home and Tell*, 42.

4. Leon Morris, *Galatians: Paul's Charter of Christian Freedom* (Downers Grove, IL: InterVarsity Press, 1996), 90.

5. Tim Keller, "Galatians: Living in Line with the Truth of the Gospel," *Gospel in Life*, 50, accessed September 8, 2022, https://gospelinlife.com/downloads/galatians-living-in-line-with-the-truth-of-the-gospel-group-study-product.

6. John Piper, "I Do Not Nullify the Grace of God," *Desiring God*, last modified March 6, 1983, https://www.desiringgod.org/messages/i-do-not-nullify-the-grace-of-god.

7. Smith, George, and George, *Go Home and Tell*, 196.

8. Smith, George, and George, *Go Home and Tell*, 196.

9. Smith, George, and George, *Go Home and Tell*, 26–27.

10. Thomas R. Schreiner, *Galatians*, Zondervan Exegetical Commentary Series, v. 9 (Grand Rapids, MI: Zondervan, 2010), 172.

11. Curtis Vaughan, *Galatians: A Study Guide* (Grand Rapids: Zondervan, 1972), 55.

12. Smith, George, and George, *Go Home and Tell*, 36–37.

13. Smith, George, and George, *Go Home and Tell*, 36.

14. Smith, George, and George, *Go Home and Tell*, 249.

15. Smith, George, and George, *Go Home and Tell*, 250.

16. Lewis Drummond, *Miss Bertha: Woman of Revival: A Biography* (Nashville, TN: B&H Pub Group, 1996), 53.

17. Drummond, *Miss Bertha*, 63–64.

18. What follows over the next few pages is a close summary of Handy's work. Wes Handy, "'An Historical Analysis of the North China Mission (SBC) and Keswick Sanctification in the Shandong Revival,' 1927–1937" (Southeastern Baptist Theological Seminary, 2012), 106–8.

19. Quoted in Handy, "An Historical Analysis," 110.

20. Quoted in Handy, "An Historical Analysis," 110.

21. Quoted in Handy, "An Historical Analysis," 111.

22. Quoted in Handy, "An Historical Analysis," 112.

23. Quoted in Handy, "An Historical Analysis," 113.

24. Quoted in Handy, "An Historical Analysis."

25. Quoted in Handy, "An Historical Analysis," 190.

26. Quoted in Handy, "An Historical Analysis," 190–91.

27. John Piper, "Only a New Creation Counts," *Desiring God*, last modified August 28, 1983, https://www.desiringgod.org/messages/only-a-new-creation-counts.

28. Smith, George, and George, *Go Home and Tell*, 97.

29. Smith, George, and George, *Go Home and Tell*, 158.

30. Smith, George, and George, *Go Home and Tell*, 163–64.

31. Smith, George, and George, *Go Home and Tell*, 200–201.

32. Smith, George, and George, *Go Home and Tell*, 273.

33. Smith, George, and George, *Go Home and Tell*, 178.

34. Smith, George, and George, *Go Home and Tell*, 262.

35. Smith, George, and George, *Go Home and Tell*, 104.

36. Smith, George, and George, *Go Home and Tell*, 110.

37. Smith, George, and George, *Go Home and Tell*, 126.

38. "Bertha Smith Legacy," *Baptist Courier*, last modified December 23, 2010, https://baptistcourier.com/2010/12/bertha-smith-legacy.

39. Don Kirkland, "Exhibit Honoring 'Miss Bertha' Opens at SBC Library & Archives," Baptist Press, February 21, 2005, https://www.baptistpress.com/resource-library/news/exhibit-honoring-miss-bertha-opens-at-sbc-library-archives.

40. Bertha Smith, "LETTER FROM CHINA, Bertha Smith: 'Unworthy of the Privilege,'" Baptist Press, August 8, 2008, https://www.baptistpress.com/resource-library/news/letter-from-china-bertha-smith-unworthy-of-the-privilege.

41. Elisabeth Elliot, *Shadow of the Almighty: The Life and Testament of Jim Elliot* (San Francisco, CA: HarperOne, 1956), 46.

Chapter 8

1. Reid S. Trulson, *Charlotte Atlee White Rowe: The Story of America's First Appointed Woman Missionary* (Macon, GA: Mercer University Press, 2021), 16. Trulson's superb work is the main and

one of the few biographical sources on Charlotte Rowe and is heavily cited in this chapter.

2. Warren W. Wiersbe, *Be Wise* (Wheaton, IL: Victor Books, 1987), 112.

3. A rare portrait of Charlotte can be seen at Reid Trulson, "Charlotte's Portrait Located," Reid Trulson, November 2, 2022, https://reidtrulson.com/charlottes-portrait-located.

4. Trulson, *Charlotte Atlee White Rowe*, 5–6.

5. Trulson, *Charlotte Atlee White Rowe*, 7.

6. Trulson, *Charlotte Atlee White Rowe*, 8.

7. Trulson, *Charlotte Atlee White Rowe*, 9.

8. Trulson, *Charlotte Atlee White Rowe*, 40–41.

9. Trulson, *Charlotte Atlee White Rowe*, 66.

10. Trulson, *Charlotte Atlee White Rowe*, 49.

11. Trulson, *Charlotte Atlee White Rowe*, 49–50.

12. Trulson, *Charlotte Atlee White Rowe*, 76.

13. Trulson, *Charlotte Atlee White Rowe*, 101–2.

14. Trulson, *Charlotte Atlee White Rowe*, 102.

15. Emphasis original; Trulson, *Charlotte Atlee White Rowe*, 95.

16. Trulson, *Charlotte Atlee White Rowe*, 103.

17. Emphasis original; Trulson, *Charlotte Atlee White Rowe*, 105.

18. Emphasis original; Trulson, *Charlotte Atlee White Rowe*, 112.

19. Trulson, *Charlotte Atlee White Rowe*, 135.

20. Trulson, *Charlotte Atlee White Rowe*, 135.

21. This was a tweet that Dr. Akin composed; https://twitter.com/DannyAkin/status/2068810033.

22. Trulson, *Charlotte Atlee White Rowe*, 123.

23. Trulson, *Charlotte Atlee White Rowe*, 127.

24. Trulson, *Charlotte Atlee White Rowe*, 131.

25. Trulson, *Charlotte Atlee White Rowe*, 143–44.

26. Trulson, *Charlotte Atlee White Rowe*, 152.

27. Trulson, *Charlotte Atlee White Rowe*, 163.

28. The quote is often attributed to Nikolaus Ludwig Count von Zinzendorf.

29. Trulson, *Charlotte Atlee White Rowe*, 195.

30. Trulson, *Charlotte Atlee White Rowe*, 195–96.

31. Trulson, *Charlotte Atlee White Rowe*, 196.

Chapter 9

1. Yvette Aarons, "Interview with Danny Akin," January 13, 2023.

2. Ray Ortlund and R. Kent Hughes, *Proverbs: Wisdom That Works* (Wheaton, IL: Crossway, 2012), 59.

3. Allen Ross, "Proverbs," in *Proverbs–Isaiah*, ed. Tremper Longman III and David E. Garland (Grand Rapids, MI: Zondervan Academic, 2008), 64–65.

4. Bruce K. Waltke, *The Book of Proverbs Chapters 1–15*, NICOT (Grand Rapids, MI: Eerdmans, 2004), 244.

5. Aarons, "Interview with Danny Akin."

6. Vesta Sauter, "Interview with Danny Akin," n.d.

7. IMB, "Yvette Aarons: Storytelling on Mission," March 5, 2021, https://www.youtube.com/watch?v=pfayc2b4niE.

8. IMB, "Yvette Aarons: Storytelling on Mission."

9. IMB, "Yvette Aarons: Storytelling on Mission."

10. Aarons, "Interview with Danny Akin."

11. Aarons, "Interview with Danny Akin."

12. Yvette Aarons, *Signs from the Sermon: The Sermon on the Mount for Deaf Readers* (Jackson, MS: DJL Ministries Inc., 1992), 10.

13. Aarons, "Interview with Danny Akin."

14. Interview with Danny Akin, August 22, 2023.

15. "Yvette Aarons," IMB, accessed April 10, 2023, https://www.imb.org/175/missionary-profiles/yvette-aarons.

16. Aarons, "Interview with Danny Akin."

17. Sauter, "Interview with Danny Akin."

18. Aarons, "Interview with Danny Akin."

19. Jonathan Akin and Daniel L. Akin, *Exalting Jesus in Proverbs* (Nashville, TN: Holman Reference, 2017), 43.

20. Ross, "Proverbs," 65.

21. United Nations, "International Day of Sign Languages: 23 September," United Nations accessed March 8, 2023, https://www.un.org/en/observances/sign-languages-day.

22. United Nations, "International Day of Sign Languages."

23. *DeafGo*, accessed April 21, 2023, https://www.deafgo.com.

24. IMB, "Fast Facts" (IMB, 2022), 4, accessed April 11, 2022, https://www.imb.org/wp-content/uploads/2022/10/fast-facts-22-deaf.pdf; Deaf Pathway Global, https://www.deafpathway.com.

25. IMB, "Fast Facts."

26. Aarons, "Interview with Danny Akin."

27. Aarons, *Signs from the Sermon*.

28. John Piper, "What Does It Mean for the Christian to Fear God?," *Desiring God*, accessed April 10, 2023, https://www.desiringgod.org/interviews/what-does-it-mean-for-the-christian-to-fear-god.

29. Ross, "Proverbs," 65.

30. "Yvette Aarons."

31. Aarons, "Interview with Danny Akin."

32. Aarons, "Interview with Danny Akin."

33. Aarons, "Interview with Danny Akin."

34. Aarons, "Interview with Danny Akin."

35. Aarons, "Interview with Danny Akin."

36. Aarons, "Interview with Danny Akin."

37. Aarons, "Interview with Danny Akin."

38. "Yvette Aarons."

39. Deaf Pathway Global, https://www.deathpathway.com.

40. "Annual Statistical Report: Reporting on 2021 Data" (IMB, May 9, 2022), 30, ahttps://www.imb.org/wp-content/uploads/2022/05/ASRDY2021-2022.05.09-Public.pdf.

41. Sauter, "Interview with Danny Akin."

42. Sauter, "Interview with Danny Akin."

43. Ken Camp, "Though Deaf, Aaron Hears the Call to Foreign Missions," *Baptist Press*, January 30, 1990, http://media.sbhla.org.s3.amazonaws.com/6915,31-Jan-1990.pdf.

44. Aarons, "Interview with Danny Akin."

Chapter 10

1. Lilias Trotter, "Quotes from the Writings of Lilias Trotter," Lilias Trotter Legacy, accessed May 6, 2023, https://liliastrotter.com/quotes.

2. I am thankful to Rebecca Pate who first brought Lilias Trotter to my attention.

3. Lisa M Sinclair, "The Legacy of Isabella Lilias Trotter," *International Bulletin of Missionary Research* 26, no. 1 (January 2002): 32.

4. Sinclair, "The Legacy of Isabella Lilias Trotter," 32.

5. I. Lilias Trotter, *Parables of the Cross: Illustrated Edition* (Moscow: Dodo Press, 2008), 4.

6. See Daniel L. Akin, "Triumphalism, Suffering and Spiritual Maturity: An Exposition of 2 Corinthians 12:1–10 in its Literary, Theological, and Historical Context." CTR 4.1 (1989), 138.

7. Miriam Huffman Rockness, *A Passion for the Impossible: The Life of Lilias Trotter* (West Lafayette, IN: Lilias Trotter Legacy, 2021), 19.

8. Sinclair, "The Legacy of Isabella Lilias Trotter," 32.

9. Sinclair, "The Legacy of Isabella Lilias Trotter," 32.

10. Rockness, *A Passion for the Impossible*, 93.

11. Trotter, "Quotes from the Writings of Lilias Trotter."

12. Trotter, "Quotes from the Writings of Lilias Trotter."

13. Lilias' artwork can be seen in her writings, her sketchbooks, and in compilations of her works. For her writings, see *Parables of the Cross and Parables of the Christ-life.* For her sketchbooks, see *Lilias Trotter's 1876 Sketchbook: Scenes from Lucerne to Venice* and *Lilias Trotter's 1889 Sketchbook: Scenes from North Africa, Italy & Switzerland.* For compilations of her works, see *A Blossom in the Desert: Reflections of Faith in the Art and Writings of Lilias Trotter; A Way of Seeing: The Inward and Outward Vision of Lilias Trotter*; and *Images of Faith: Reflections Inspired by Lilias Trotter.* To order her books, go to https://liliastrotter.com/writingart.

14. Rockness, *A Passion for the Impossible*, 70.

15. Rockness, *A Passion for the Impossible*, 71.

16. Rockness, *A Passion for the Impossible*, 83.

17. Rockness, *A Passion for the Impossible*, 84.

18. Trotter, *Parables of the Cross*, 17–19. Emphasis original.

19. Trotter, *Parables of the Cross*, 22. Emphasis original.

20. Trotter, *Parables of the Cross*, 8. Emphasis original.

21. Trotter, *Parables of the Cross*, 14. Emphasis original.

22. Trotter, *Parables of the Cross*, 15. Emphasis original.

23. Trotter, *Parables of the Cross*, 20–21. Emphasis original.

24. Trotter, "Quotes from the Writings of Lilias Trotter."

25. Elisabeth Elliot, *Shadow of the Almighty: The Life and Testament of Jim Elliot* (San Francisco, CA: HarperOne, 1956), 46.

26. Rebecca Pate, "An Unconscious Greatness: Lilias Trotter as a Trailblazing Missionary, 1888–1928" (Wake Forest, NC: Southeastern Baptist Theological Seminary, 2022), 10.

27. Sinclair, "The Legacy of Isabella Lilias Trotter," 33.

28. Constance Evelyn Padwick, "Lilias Trotter of Algiers," *International Review of Mission* 21, no. 1 (January 1932): 123.

29. Sinclair, "The Legacy of Isabella Lilias Trotter," 35, n. 14.

30. Constance Evelyn Padwick, The Master of the Impossible: Sayings, for the *Most Part in Parable, from the Letters and Journals of Lilias Trotter of Algiers* (London: Society for Promoting Christian Knowledge, 1938), 194.

31. Quoted in Pate, "An Unconscious Greatness," 11–12.

32. Quoted in Pate, "An Unconscious Greatness," 12.

33. Quoted in Pate, "An Unconscious Greatness," 14.

34. Rockness, *A Passion for the Impossible*, 326–27.

35. Rockness, *A Passion for the Impossible*, 327.

36. Rockness, *A Passion for the Impossible*, 324.

37. Rockness, *A Passion for the Impossible*, 324.

38. *The Baptist Hymnal* (Nashville, TN: Convention Press, 1991).